The Psychol

MW01241161

by David C. Taylor

To My Mother

WHOSE DEVOTION TO TRUTH AND EARNEST LABOR HAS PROMPTED ALL MY
EFFORTS THIS WORK IS AFFECTIONATELY DEDICATED

A peculiar gap exists between the accepted theoretical basis of instruction in singing and the actual methods of vocal teachers. Judging by the number of scientific treatises on the voice, the academic observer would be led to believe that a coherent Science of Voice Culture has been evolved. Modern methods of instruction in singing are presumed to embody a system of exact and infallible rules for the management of the voice. Teachers of singing in all the musical centers of Europe and America claim to follow a definite plan in the training of voices, based on established scientific principles. But a practical acquaintance with the modern art of Voice Culture reveals the fact that the laws of tone-production deduced from the scientific investigation of the voice do not furnish a satisfactory basis for a method of training voices.

Throughout the entire vocal profession, among singers, teachers, and students alike, there is a general feeling of the insufficiency of present knowledge of the voice. The problem of the correct management of the vocal organs has not been finally and definitely solved. Voice Culture has not been reduced to an exact science. Vocal teachers are not in possession of an infallible method of training voices. Students of singing find great difficulty in learning how to use their voices. Voice Culture is generally recognized as entitled to a position among the exact sciences; but something remains to be done before it can assume that position.

There must be some definite reason for the failure of theoretical investigation to produce a satisfactory Science of Voice Culture. This cannot be due to any present lack of understanding of the vocal mechanism on the part of scientific students of the subject. The anatomy and physiology of the vocal organs have been exhaustively studied by a vast number of highly trained experts. So far as the muscular operations of tone-production are concerned, and the laws of acoustics bearing on the vocal action, no new discovery can well be expected. But in this very fact, the exhaustive attention paid to the mechanical operations of the voice, is seen the incompleteness of Vocal Science. Attention has been turned exclusively to the mechanical features of tone-production, and in consequence many important facts bearing on the voice have been overlooked.

In spite of the general acceptance of the doctrines of Vocal Science, tone-production has not really been studied from the purely scientific standpoint. The use of the word "science" presupposes the careful observation and study of all facts and phenomena bearing in any way on the subject investigated. Viewed in this light, the scientific study of the voice is at once seen to be incomplete. True, the use of the voice is a muscular operation, and a knowledge of the muscular structure of the vocal organs is necessary to an understanding of the voice. But this knowledge alone is not sufficient. Like every other voluntary muscular operation, tone-production is subject to the psychological laws of control and guidance. Psychology is therefore of equal importance with anatomy and acoustics as an element of Vocal Science.

There is also another line along which all previous investigation of the voice is singularly incomplete. An immense fund of information about the vocal action is obtained by attentive listening to voices, and in no other way. Yet this important element in Vocal Science is almost completely neglected.

In order to arrive at an assured basis for the art of Voice Culture, it is necessary in the first place to apply the strictest rules of scientific investigation to the study of the voice. A definite plan must be adopted, to include every available source information. First, the insight into the operations of the voice, obtained by listening to voices, must be reviewed and analyzed. Second, the sciences of anatomy, mechanics, acoustics, and psychology must each contribute its share to the general fund of information. Third, from all the facts thus brought together the general laws of vocal control and management must be deduced.

Before undertaking this exhaustive analysis of the vocal action it is advisable to review in detail every method of instruction in singing now in vogue. This may seem a very difficult task. To the casual observer conditions in the vocal world appear truly chaotic. Almost every prominent teacher believes himself to possess a method peculiarly his own; it would not be easy to find two masters who agree on every point, practical as well as theoretical. But this confusion of methods is only on the surface. All teachers draw the materials of their methods from the same sources. An outline of the history of Voice Culture, including the rise of the old Italian school and the development of Vocal Science, will render the present situation in the vocal profession sufficiently clear. Part I of this work contains a review of modern methods. In Part II a critical analysis is offered of certain theories of the vocal action which receive much attention in practical instruction. Several of the accepted doctrines of Vocal Science, notably those of breath-control, chest and nasal resonance, and forward placing of the tone, are found on examination to contain serious fallacies. More important even than the specific errors involved in these doctrines, the basic principle of modern Voice Culture is also found to be false. All methods are based on the theory that the voice requires to be directly and consciously managed in the performance of its muscular operations. When tested by the psychological laws of muscular guidance, this theory of mechanical tone-production is found to be a complete error. Part III contains a summary of all present knowledge of the voice.

First, the insight into the singer's vocal operations is considered, which the hearer obtains by attentive listening to the tones produced. This empirical knowledge, as it is generally called, indicates a state of unnecessary throat tension as the cause, or at any rate the accompaniment, of every faulty tone. Further, an outline is given of all scientific knowledge of the voice. The anatomy of the vocal organs, and the acoustic and mechanical principles of the vocal action, are briefly described. Finally, the psychological laws of tone-production are considered. It is seen that under normal conditions the voice instinctively obeys the commands of the ear. In Part IV the information about the vocal action obtained from the two sources is combined,--the scientific knowledge of mechanical processes, and the empirical knowledge derived from attentive listening to voices. Throat stiffness is then seen to be the one influence which can interfere with the instinctively correct action of the voice. The most important cause of throat stiffness is found in the attempt consciously to manage the mechanical operations of the voice. In place of the erroneous principles of mechanical instruction, imitation is seen to be the rational foundation of a method of Voice Culture. The mystery surrounding the old Italian method is dispelled so soon as the possibility is recognized of teaching singing by imitation. Practical rules are outlined for imparting and acquiring the correct use of the voice, through the guidance of the sense of hearing. The singer's education is considered in its broadest sense, and training in tone-production is assigned to its proper place in the complex scheme of Voice Culture.

During the past twenty years the author has found opportunity to hear most of the famous singers who have visited America, as well as a host of artists of somewhat lesser fame. In his early student days the conviction grew that the voice cannot reach its fullest development when mechanically used. Siegfried does not forge his sword, and at the same time think of his diaphragm or soft palate. Lucia cannot attend to the movements of her arytenoid cartilages while pouring out the trills and runs of her Mad Scene. A study of the theoretical works on Vocal Science, dealing always with mechanical action and never with tone, served only to strengthen this conviction. Finally the laws of physiological psychology were found to confirm this early belief.

Every obtainable work on Voice Culture has been included in the author's reading. No desire must be understood to make a display of the results of this study. One citation from a recognized authority, or in some cases two or three, is held sufficient to verify each statement regarding the accepted doctrines of Vocal Science. As for the practical features of modern methods, the facts alleged cannot in every case be substantiated by references to published works. It is, however, believed that the reader's acquaintance with the subject will bear out the author's statements.

This work is of necessity academic in conception and in substance. Its only purpose is to demonstrate the falsity of the idea of mechanical vocal management, and to prove the scientific soundness of instruction by imitation. There is no possibility of a practical manual of instruction in singing being accepted, based on the training of the ear and the musical education of the singer, until the vocal world has been convinced of the error of the mechanical idea. When that has been accomplished this work will have served its purpose. All of the controversial materials, together with much of the theoretical subject matter, will then be superfluous. A concise practical treatise can then be offered, containing all that the vocal teacher and the student of singing need to know about the training and management of the voice.

It is in great measure due to the cooperation of my dear friend, Charles Leonard-Stuart, that my theory of voice production is brought into literary form, and presented in this book. To his thorough musicianship, his skill and experience as a writer of English, and especially to his mastery of the bookman's art, I am deeply indebted. True as I know Leonard-Stuart's love to be for the art of pure singing, I yet prefer to ascribe his unselfish interest in this work to his friendship for the author.

CONTENTS

The Disappearance of the Old Italian Method and the Development of Mechanical Instruction

CHAPTER VIII

The Materials of Rational Instruction in Singing

CHAPTER IX

Outlines of a Practical Method of Voice Culture

Bibliography

CHAPTER I

TONE-PRODUCTION AND VOICE CULTURE

In no other form of expression do art and nature seem so closely identified as in the art of singing. A perfect voice speaks so directly to the soul of the hearer that all appearance of artfully prepared effect is absent. Every tone sung by a consummate vocal artist seems to be poured forth freely and spontaneously. There is no evidence of calculation, of carefully directed effort, of attention to the workings of the voice, in the tones of a perfect singer. Yet if the accepted idea of Voice Culture is correct, this semblance of spontaneity in the use of the voice can result only from careful and incessant attention to mechanical rules. That the voice must be managed or handled in some way neither spontaneous nor instinctive, is the settled conviction of almost every authority on the subject. All authorities believe also that this manner of handling the voice must be acquired by every student of singing, in the course of carefully directed study.

This training in the use of the voice is the most important feature of education in singing. Voice Culture embraces a peculiar and distinct problem, that of the correct management of the vocal organs. Vocal training has indeed come to be considered synonymous with training in the correct use of the voice. Every method of instruction in singing must contain as its most important element some means for dealing with the problem of tone-production.

No complete and satisfactory solution of this problem has ever been found. Of this fact every one acquainted with the practical side of Voice Culture must be well aware. As the present work is designed solely to suggest a new manner of dealing with this question, it is advisable to define precisely what is meant by the problem of tone-production.

In theory the question may be stated very simply. It is generally believed throughout the vocal profession that the voice has one correct mode of action, different from a wide variety of incorrect actions of which it is capable;--that this mode of action, though ordained by Nature, is not in the usual sense natural or instinctive;--that the correct vocal action must be acquired, through a definite understanding and conscious management of the muscular movements involved. The theoretical problem therefore is: What is the correct vocal action, and how can it be acquired?

On the practical side, the nature of the problem is by no means so simple. In actual instruction in singing, the subject of vocal management cannot readily be dissociated from the wide range of other topics comprised in the singer's education. In much that pertains to the art of music, the singer's training must include the same subjects that form the training of every musician. In addition to this general musical training, about the same for all students of music, each student must acquire technical command of the chosen instrument. This is necessarily acquired by practice on the instrument, whether it be piano, violin, oboe, or whatever else. In the same way, vocal technique is acquired by practice in actual singing. Practice makes perfect, with the voice as with everything else.

But the voice is not invariably subject to the law that practice makes perfect. In this important respect the singer's education presents a problem not encountered by the student of any instrument. Given the necessary talents, industry, and opportunities for study, the student of the violin may count with certainty on acquiring the mastery of this instrument. But for the vocal student this is not necessarily true. There are many cases in which practice in singing does not bring about technical perfection. The mere singing of technical exercises is not enough; it is of vital importance that the exercises be sung in some particular manner. There is one certain way in which the voice must be handled during the practice of singing. If the vocal organs are exercised in this particular manner, the voice will improve steadily as the result of practice. This progress will continue until perfect technical command of the voice is acquired. But if the vocal student fails to hit upon this particular way of handling the voice in practice the voice will improve little, or not at all. In such a case perfect vocal technique will never be acquired, no matter how many years the practice may continue.

What is this peculiar way in which the voice must be handled during the practice of singing? This is the practical problem of tone-production, as it confronts the student of singing.

It is important that the exact bearing of the problem be clearly understood. It is purely a feature of education in singing, and concerns only teachers and students of the art. Properly speaking, the finished singer should leave the teacher and start on the artistic career, equipped with a voice under perfect control. There should be no problem of tone-production for the trained singer, no thought or worry about the vocal action. True, many authorities on the voice maintain that the artist must, in all singing, consciously and intelligently guide the operations of the vocal organs. But even if this be the case the fact remains that this ability to manage the voice must be acquired during student days. In seeking a solution of the problem, that period in the prospective singer's training must be considered during which the proper use of the voice is learned.

It may be taken for granted that teachers of singing have always been aware of the existence of the problem of tone-production, and have always instructed their pupils in the correct management of the voice. Yet it is only within the past hundred and fifty years that vocal management has been the subject of special study. A brief review of the history of Voice Culture will serve to bring this fact out clearly.

To begin with, the present art of singing is of comparatively recent origin. It is indeed probable that man had been using the voice in something akin to song for thousands of years before the dawn of history. Song of some kind has always played an important part in human life, savage as well as civilized. To express our emotions and feelings by means of the voice is one of our most deep-seated instincts. For this use of the voice to take on the character of melody, as distinguished from ordinary speech, is also purely instinctive. Singing was one of the most zealously cultivated arts in early Egypt, in ancient Israel, and in classic Greece and Rome. Throughout all the centuries of European history singing has always had its recognized place, both in the services of the various churches and in the daily life of the people.

But solo singing, as we know it to-day, is a comparatively modern art. Not until the closing decades of the sixteenth century did the art of solo singing receive much attention, and it is to that period we must look for the beginnings of Voice Culture. It is true that the voice was cultivated, both for speech and song, among the Greeks and Romans. Gordon Holmes, in his Treatise on Vocal Physiology and Hygiene (London, 1879), gives an interesting account of these ancient systems of Voice Culture. But practically nothing has come down to us about the means then used for training the voice. Even if any defined methods were developed, it is absolutely certain that these had no influence on the modern art of Voice Culture.

With the birth of Italian opera, in 1600, a new art of singing also came into existence. The two arts, opera and singing, developed side by side, each dependent on the other. And most important to the present inquiry, the art or science of training voices also came into being. In Le Revoluzioni del Teatro Musicale Italiano (Venice, 1785), Arteaga says of the development of opera: "But nothing contributed so much to clarify Italian music at that time as the excellence and the abundance of the singers." A race of singing masters seems almost to have sprung up in Italy. These illustrious masters taught the singers to produce effects with their voices such as had never been heard of before. From 1600 to 1750 the progress of the art of singing was uninterrupted. Each great teacher carried the art a little further, discovering new beauties and powers in the voice, and finding means to impart his new knowledge to his pupils.

This race of teachers is known to-day as the Old Italian School, and their system of instruction is called the Old Italian Method. Just what this method consisted of is a much-discussed question. Whatever its system of instruction, the old Italian school seems to have suffered a gradual decline. In 1800 it was distinctly on the wane; it was entirely superseded, during the years from 1840 to 1865, by the modern scientific methods.

Considered as a practical system of Voice Culture, the old Italian method is a highly mysterious subject. Little is now known about the means used for training students of singing in the correct use of the voice. This much is fairly certain: the old masters paid little or no attention to what are now considered scientific principles. They taught in what modern vocal theorists consider a rather haphazard fashion. The term "empirical" is often applied to their method, and to the knowledge of the voice on which it was based.[1] But as to what the old masters actually knew about the voice, and just how they taught their pupils to sing, on these points the modern world is in almost complete ignorance. Many attempts have been made in recent years to reconstruct the old Italian method in the light of modern scientific knowledge of the voice. But no such analysis of the empirical system has ever been convincing.

[Note 1: "The old Italian method of instruction, to which vocal music owed its high condition, was purely empirical." (Emma Seiler, The Voice in Singing. Phila., 1886.)]

How the practical method of the old masters came to be forgotten is perhaps the most mysterious feature of this puzzling system. There has been a lineal succession of teachers of singing, from the earlier decades of the eighteenth century down to the present. Even to-day it is almost unheard of that any one should presume to call himself a teacher of singing without having studied with at least one recognized master. Each master of the old school imparted his knowledge and his practical method to his pupils. Those of his pupils who in their turn became teachers passed the method on to their students, and so on, in many unbroken successions. Yet, for some mysterious reason, the substance of the old method was lost in transmission.

What little is now known about the old method is derived from two sources, the written record and tradition. To write books in explanation of their system of instruction does not seem to have occurred to the earliest exponents of the art of Voice Culture. The first published work on the subject was that of Pietro Francesco Tosi, Osservazione sopra il Canto figurato, brought out in Bologna in 1723. This was translated into English by M. Galliard, and published in London in 1742; a German translation by J. F. Agricola was issued in 1757. The present work will call for several citations from Tosi, all taken from the English edition. Only one other prominent teacher of the old school, G. B. Mancini, has left an apparently complete record of his method. His Riflessioni pratiche sul Canto figurato was published in Milan in 1776. Mancini's book has never been translated into English. Reference will therefore be made to the third Italian edition, brought out in Milan, 1777.

Tosi and Mancini undoubtedly intended to give complete accounts of the methods of instruction in singing in vogue in their day. But modern vocal theorists generally believe that the most important materials of instruction were for some reason not mentioned. Three registers are mentioned by Tosi, while Mancini speaks of only two. Both touch on the necessity of equalizing the registers, but give no specific directions for this purpose. About all these early writers have left us, in the opinion of most modern students of their works, is the outline of an elaborate system of vocal ornaments and embellishments.

On the side of tradition a slightly more coherent set of rules has come down to us from the old masters. These are generally known as the "traditional precepts." Just when the precepts were first formulated it is impossible to say. Tosi and Mancini do not mention them. Perhaps they were held by the old masters as a sort of esoteric mystery; this idea is occasionally put forward. At any rate, by the time the traditional precepts were given to the world in published works on the voice, their valuable meaning had been completely lost.

Gathered from all available sources, the traditional precepts are as follows:

"Sing on the breath."

"Open the throat."

"Sing the tone forward," or "at the lips."

"Support the tone."

To the layman these precepts are so vague as to be almost unintelligible. But modern vocal teachers are convinced that the precepts sum up the most important means used by the old masters for imparting the correct vocal action. An interpretation of the precepts in terms intelligible to the modern student would therefore be extremely valuable. Many scientific investigators of the voice have sought earnestly to discover the sense in which the precepts were applied by the old masters. These explanations of the traditional precepts occupy a very important position in most modern methods of instruction.

There can be no question that the old masters were highly successful teachers of singing. Even leaving out of consideration the vocal achievements of the castrati, the singers of Tosi's day must have been able to perform music of the florid style in a masterly fashion. This is plainly seen from a study of the scores of the operas popular at that time. Empirical methods of instruction seem to have sufficed for the earlier masters. Not until the old method had been in existence for nearly one hundred and fifty years does an attempt seem to have been made to study the voice scientifically. In 1741 a famous French physician, Ferrein, published a treatise on the vocal organs. This was the first scientific work to influence the practices of vocal teachers.

For many years after the publication of Ferrein's treatise, the scientific study of the voice attracted very little attention from the singing masters. Fully sixty years elapsed before any serious attempt was made to base a method of instruction on scientific principles. Even then the idea of scientific instruction in singing gained ground very slowly. Practical teachers at first paid but little attention to the subject. Interest in the mechanics of voice production was confined almost entirely to the scientists.

In the early decades of the nineteenth century the mechanical features of voice production seem to have appealed to a constantly wider circle of scientists. Lickovius (1814), Malgaine (1831), Bennati (1830), Bell (1832), Savart (1825), brought out works on the subject. It remained, however, for a vocal teacher, Garcia, to conceive the idea of basing practical instruction on scientific knowledge.

Manuel Garcia (1805-1906) may justly be regarded as the founder of Vocal Science. His father, Manuel del Popolo Viscenti, was famous as singer, impresario, and teacher. From him Garcia inherited the old method, it is safe to assume, in its entirety. But for Garcia's remarkable mind the empirical methods of the old school were unsatisfactory. He desired definite knowledge of the voice. A clear idea seems to have been in his mind that, with full understanding of the vocal mechanism and of its correct mode of action, voices would be more readily and surely trained. How strongly this idea had possession of Garcia is shown by the fact that he began the study of the vocal action in 1832, and that he invented the laryngoscope only in 1855.

It must not be understood that Garcia was the first teacher to attempt to formulate a systematic scheme of instruction in singing. In the works of Mannstein (1834) and of Marx (1823) an ambitious forward movement on the part of many prominent teachers is strongly indicated. But Garcia was the first teacher to apply scientific principles in dealing with the specific problem of tone-production. He conceived the idea that a scientific knowledge of the workings of the vocal organs might be made the basis of a practical system or method of instruction in singing. This idea of Garcia has been the basic principle of all practical methods, ever since the publication of the results of his first laryngoscopic investigations in 1855.

Before attempting to suggest a new means of dealing with the problem of vocal management, it is well to ascertain how this problem is treated in modern methods of instruction. It would not be easy to overstate the importance assigned to the matter of tone-production in all modern systems of Voice Culture. The scientific study of the voice has dealt exclusively with this subject. A new science has resulted, commonly called "Vocal Science." This science is generally accepted as the foundation of all instruction in singing. All modern methods are to some extent based on Vocal Science.

To arrive at an understanding of modern methods, the two directions in which vocal theorists have approached the scientific study of the voice must be borne in mind: First, by an investigation of the anatomy of the vocal organs, and of the laws of acoustics and mechanics in accordance with which they operate. Second, by an analysis of the traditional precepts of the old Italian school in the light of this scientific knowledge.

As the present work demands a review of modern methods from the practical side only, it is not necessary to include a description of the vocal organs. It will be sufficient to describe briefly the manner in which scientific investigators of the voice treat the subject of the vocal organs.

The vocal mechanism consists of three portions,--the breathing apparatus, the larynx with its appendages, and the resonance cavities. Vocal scientists apply their efforts to finding out the correct mode of action of each portion of the mechanism, and to formulating rules and exercises by which these correct actions can be acquired and combined for the production of perfect tones. The analysis of the traditional precepts also conforms to this general plan; each precept is referred to that portion of the vocal apparatus to which it seems best to apply. The outline of the principles of modern methods contained in the following chapters follows this general scheme.

It must be understood at the start that on most of the doctrines included in Vocal Science there is no unanimity of opinion among either theorists or teachers. Far from this being the case, practically all the principles of Vocal Science are the subjects of controversy.

CHAPTER II

BREATHING AND BREATH-CONTROL

It is generally considered that, as the breath is the foundation of singing, the manner of breathing is of vital importance to the singer. This subject has therefore received a vast amount of attention from vocal scientists, and the muscular actions of breathing have been exhaustively studied.

Several sets of rules for inspiration and expiration are put forth by different authorities. But there is no occasion for going into a detailed discussion of the different modes of breathing advocated by the various schools, or of the theoretical arguments which each advances. It is sufficient to say that the modes of breathing most in vogue are five in number,--deep abdominal, lateral or costal, fixed high chest, clavicular, and diaphragmatic-abdominal. However, on experimenting with these five systems of breathing, it is found that the number may be reduced to two; of these the others are but slight modifications. In one system of inspiration the abdomen is protruded, while the upper chest is held firm, the greatest expansion being at the base of the lungs. In the other mode of taking breath the abdomen is slightly drawn in, while the chest is expanded in every direction, upward, laterally, forward, and backward. In this system the upper chest is held in a fixed and high position.

Necessarily the manner of filling the lungs involves the manner in which they are emptied. Opinions are practically unanimous as to the proper position of the singer before taking breath, that is, at the end of an expiration. The singer must stand erect, the weight of the body evenly supported on the balls of both feet, with the whole body in a condition of lithe suppleness. In both systems of breathing the manner of expiration is simply a return to this position.

A wide variety of breathing exercises are in use, but these do not require detailed description. Any one of the prescribed systems of breathing can easily be adopted, and the student of singing seldom encounters any difficulty on this point. Still most teachers attach great importance to the acquirement of the correct manner of breathing. Toneless mechanical exercises are generally given, by which the student is expected to master the muscular movements before applying in singing the system advocated by the teacher. These exercises are usually combined with those for breath-control, and they are described under that head.

Breath-Control

Very early in the development of Vocal Science the management of the breath began to receive attention. Mannstein,[2] writing in 1834, says: "The air in expiration must stream from the chest slowly and without shock. The air must flow from the chest with the tone." In a footnote he adds: "In order to acquire this economy of the breath, students were required to practise daily, without singing, to take and to hold back the breath as long as possible." Mannstein does not mention the muscular action involved in this exercise.

[Note 2: Die grosse italienische Gesangschule. Dresden, 1834.]

This subject is also touched upon by Garcia. In the first edition of his de Garcia, 1847, Chap. IV, p. 14, he says: "The mechanism of expiration consists of a gentle pressure on the lungs charged with air, operated by the thorax and the diaphragm. The shock of the chest, the sudden falling of the ribs, and the quick relaxing of the diaphragm cause the air to escape instantly.... If, while the lungs are filled with air, the ribs are allowed to fall, and the diaphragm to rise, the lungs instantly give up the inspired air, like a pressed sponge. It is necessary therefore to allow the ribs to fall and the diaphragm to relax only so much as is required to sustain the tones." It may be questioned whether Garcia had in mind the doctrine of breath-control as this is understood to-day. Very little attention was paid, at any rate, in the vocal instruction of that day, to the mechanical actions of breath-control; the great majority of teachers probably had never heard of this principle.

As a definite principle of Vocal Science, breath-control was first formulated by Dr. Mandl, in his Die Gesundheitslehre der Stimme, Brunswick, 1876. From that time on, this doctrine has been very generally recognized as the fundamental principle of correct singing. Practically every scientific writer on the voice since then states breath-control as one of the basic principles of Vocal Science. The most influential published work in popularizing the doctrine of breath-control was probably the book written jointly by Lennox Browne and Emil Behnke, Voice, Song, and Speech, London, 1883.

This doctrine is of so much importance in Vocal Science and in modern methods of instruction as to require a detailed explanation. The theory of breath-control may be stated as follows:[3]

"In ordinary breathing the air is expelled from the lungs quietly, but rapidly; at no point of the breathing apparatus does the expired breath meet with resistance. In singing, on the contrary, the expiratory pressure is much more powerful, yet the expiration must be much slower. Furthermore, all the expired breath must be converted into tone, and the singer must have perfect control over the strength and the speed of the expiration. This requires that the air be held back at some point. The action of holding back the breath must not be performed by the muscles which close the glottis, for all the muscles of the larynx are very small and weak in comparison with the powerful muscles of expiration. The glottis-closing muscles are too weak to oppose their action to the force of a powerful expiration. If the vocal cords are called upon to withstand a strong breath pressure, they are seriously strained, and their proper action is rendered impossible. In the same way, if the throat be narrowed at any point above the larynx, so as to present a passage small enough to hold back a powerful expiration, the entire vocal mechanism is strained and forced out of its proper adjustment. The singer must have perfect control of the breath, and at the same time relieve the larynx and throat of all pressure and strain. To obtain this control the singer must govern the expiration by means of the muscles of inspiration. When the lungs are filled the inspiratory muscles are not to be relaxed as in ordinary breathing, but are to be held on tension throughout the action of expiration. Whatever pressure is exerted by the expiratory muscles must be almost counterbalanced by the opposed action of the muscles of inspiration. The more powerful the blast, the greater must be the exertion by which it is controlled. In this way the singer may have perfect control both of the speed and of the strength of the expiration."

[Note 3: This statement of the doctrine of breath-control must not be construed as an endorsement of the theory of the vocal action embodied in this doctrine. On the contrary, both the theory of "opposed action" breath-control and the "breath-band" theory are held to be utterly erroneous. For a further discussion of this subject see Chapter II of Part II.]

The exercises for acquiring command of this "opposed action breath-control" are easily understood; indeed, they will readily suggest themselves to one who has grasped their purpose. Most important of these exercises is a quick inspiration, followed by a slow and controlled expiration. Exercises for breathing and breath-control are usually combined; the student is instructed to take breath in the manner advocated by the teacher, and then to control the expiration.

Teachers usually require their pupils to obtain command of this action as a toneless exercise before permitting them to apply it to the production of tone. Methods vary greatly as to the length of time devoted to toneless drills in breathing and breath-control. Many teachers demand that students practise these exercises daily throughout the entire course of study, and even recommend that this practice be continued throughout the singer's active life.

Simple as these exercises are in theory, they demand very arduous practice. Control of the breath by "opposed action" is hard and tiring muscular work, as the reader may easily convince himself by practising the above described exercise for a few minutes.

No special rules are needed for applying this mode of breathing to the production of tone. Theoretical writers generally do not claim that the control of the breath brings about the correct laryngeal action, but merely that it permits this action by noninterference. Several authorities however, notably Shakespeare, maintain that in effect this system of breath-control embodies the old precept, "Sing on the breath." (Wm. Shakespeare, The Art of Singing, London, 1898, p. 24.) Other theorists hold that the empirical precept, "Support the tone," refers to this manner of controlled expiration. (G. B. Lamperti, The Technics of Bel Canto, Trans. by Dr. Th. Baker, N. Y., 1905, p. 9.)

The "Breath-band" System

While most authorities on the voice advocate the system of breath-control by "opposed muscular action," there are a number of masters who teach an entirely different system. This is usually known as the "Breath-band," or "Ventricular" breath-control. Charles Lunn, in The Philosophy of the Voice, 1878, was the first to propound the theory that the breath may be controlled by the false vocal cords. There is reason to believe that this idea was also worked out independently by Orlando Steed ("On Beauty of Touch and Tone," Proceedings of the Musical Assn., 1879-80, p. 47). As a number of prominent teachers base their entire methods on this theory, it is worthy of careful attention. The "breath-band" theory may be stated as follows:

"When the lungs are filled by a deep inspiration and the breath is held, the glottis is of necessity closed so tightly that no air can escape. In this condition the expiratory muscles may be very violently contracted, and still no air will escape; indeed, the greater the strength exerted the tighter is the closure of the glottis. Obviously, this closure of the glottis cannot be effected by the contraction of the glottis-closing muscles, strictly speaking, for these muscles are too small and weak to withstand the powerful air pressure exerted against the vocal cords.[4] The point of resistance is located just above the vocal cords. The sudden air pressure exerted on the interior walls of the larynx by the expiratory contraction causes the ventricles of the larynx to expand by inflation. This inflation of the ventricles brings their upper margins, formed by the false vocal cords, into contact. Thus the opening from the larynx into the pharynx is closed. This closure is not effected by any muscular contraction, therefore it is not dependent on the strength of the muscular fibers of the false vocal cords. It is an automatic valvular action, directly under voluntary control so far as the contraction of the expiratory muscles is concerned, but independent of volition as regards the action of the false vocal cords. On account of their important function in this operation the false vocal cords are called the 'breath-bands.' Closure of the glottis by the inflation of the ventricles imposes no strain on the vocal cords.

[Note 4: One of the strongest arguments of the "breath-band" advocates is based on this action,--the resistance of the closed glottis to a powerful expiratory pressure. The theory of breath-control by "opposed muscular action" takes no cognizance of this operation. It will however be shown in Chapter II of

Part II that the "breath-band"

theorists are mistaken in asserting that the action of holding the breath is not performed by the glottis-closing muscles.]

"Control of the breath in singing is effected by this automatic valvular action. To produce a tone according to this system, the lungs must be filled and the breath held in the manner just described, while the vocal cords are brought to the proper degree of tension; then the tone is started by allowing the 'breath-bands' to separate very slightly, so that a thin stream of air is forced through the opening between their margins. The tone is ushered in by a slight explosive sound, which is nothing but the well-known stroke of the glottis. So long as the expiratory pressure is steadily maintained, this tone may be held, and yet no strain is imposed on the vocal cords. Perfect control of the breath is thus attained. For a powerful tone, the breath blast is greater, therefore the ventricles are more widely inflated, and the opening between the 'breath-bands' becomes narrower. The action is always automatic; once the tone is correctly started, the singer need pay no further attention to the operation of the 'breath-bands.' All that is necessary is to maintain a steady breath pressure."

In the methods of all the "breath-band" advocates, the first and most important step toward perfect tone-production is held to be the acquirement of this automatic breath-control. As in the "opposed muscular" system, the initial exercises are toneless drills in breathing. The basic exercise, of which all the others are variations, is as follows: "Fill the lungs, then hold the breath an instant, and forcibly contract all the chest muscles. Then force the air out slowly and powerfully through the glottis." Practice of this exercise is always accompanied by a hissing sound, caused by the escape of the air through the narrow slit between (presumably) the "breath-bands." Tone-production by the same muscular action is very simple, and requires no further explanation.

In its practical aspect this system of breath-control is the direct opposite of the "opposed muscular" system. In one the breath is expelled powerfully, the object being to bring a strong expiratory pressure to bear on the larynx. In the other system, the air is held back, in order that the larynx be exposed to as slight a pressure as possible.

The "breath-band" advocates hold that the glottic stroke is the key to correct laryngeal action. As a rule they instruct their pupils to attack every tone, throughout all their practising, with the stroke of the glottis. In the course of time the automatic valvular action is supposed to become so well established that the singer can dispense with the glottic stroke in public performance. Needless to say, these teachers usually recognize that this explosive sound is very harsh and unmusical, and utterly out of place in artistic singing.

An important claim of the "breath-band" teachers is that their doctrine contains the explanation of the traditional precept, "Support the tone." Their idea is that the throat, being "firmly set," furnishes a secure base for the tone to rest on. This explanation is of course utterly unscientific, and it cannot be said to throw any light on the meaning of the precept. "Singing on the breath" is also referred to this system of breath-control, but with no more coherence than the "Support of the tone."

No necessary connection obtains between systems of breath-control and those of breathing strictly speaking, that is, of inspiration. As has been said, the great majority of vocal theorists adhere to the "opposed muscular action" breath-control. In this number are included advocates of every known system of breathing. Bitter controversies have been carried on between champions of different modes of breathing, who yet agree that the breath must be controlled by "opposed action." This is also true, although not to the same extent, among the "breath-band" teachers. And to render the confusion on the subject of breathing and breath-control complete, instances might be cited of controversies between teachers who agree as to the correct mode of inspiration, and yet disagree on the manner of controlling the expiration.

Both systems of breath-control cannot be right; if one is correct, the other must necessarily be absolutely wrong. Instead of attempting to decide between them, it will be seen that both are false, and that the theory on which they rest is erroneous. This discussion is reserved for a later chapter.

CHAPTER III

REGISTERS AND LARYNGEAL ACTION

Probably no other topic of Vocal Science has been studied so earnestly as the registers of the voice. Yet on no other topic is there such wide diversity of opinion among theorists and investigators.

Very little is definitely known regarding the manner in which the subject of registers was treated by the old Italian masters. Suffice it to say here that the old masters did not refer the registers to changes in the laryngeal action. They were treated simply as different qualities of tone, each quality best adapted to be sung only in a portion of the voice's compass.

In the early decades of the nineteenth century the registers of the voice received much attention from vocal theorists, especially in Paris. Garcia's first published work, M 鬧 oire sur la Voix humaine, was presented to the Academy of Sciences in 1840. This M 鬧 oire gives the results of observations which Garcia made on his own pupils; it deals mainly with the position of the larynx during the singing of tones in the various registers. Garcia describes how the larynx is raised and lowered in the throat, according to the register in which the tones are produced. He also notes the position of the tongue and the soft palate.

Widespread interest was awakened by the account of Garcia's laryngoscopic investigations of the registers, published in 1855. The attention of the great majority of vocalists was at once drawn to the subject, and the actions of the vocal cords in the different registers were studied by many prominent physicians and voice specialists. Exhaustive treatises on the registers have since been published by Mme. Seiler, Behnke, Curwen, Mills, Battaille, Curtis, Holmes, and by a large number of other investigators.

All the results of the laryngoscopic investigation of the vocal action have been disappointing in the extreme. In the first place, no two observers have obtained exactly the same results. Writing in 1886, Sir Morell Mackenzie says: "Direct observation with the laryngoscope is, of course, the best method at our disposal, but that even its testimony is far from unexceptionable is obvious from the marvelous differences as to matters of fact that exist among observers. It is hardly too much to say that no two of them quite agree as to what is seen." (The Hygiene of the Vocal Organs, London, 1886.) Wesley Mills, in his latest work, endeavors to show a substantial agreement among the best equipped observers of the registers, but his attempt can hardly be called convincing. (Voice Production in Singing and Speaking, Philadelphia, 1906.) Opinions on the subject of registers, held by the leading voice specialists to-day, are fully as divergent as in 1886. Widely different statements are made by prominent authorities as to the number of registers, the vocal cord action by which each register is produced, and the number of notes which each one should properly include.

Another deficiency of the doctrine of registers is even more serious in its bearing on practical instruction. Not only have all investigators failed to define exactly what the correct laryngeal action is. Even if this were determined it would still be necessary to find means for imparting command of this correct action to the student of singing. Knowing how the vocal cords should act does not help the singer in the least to govern their action. What the vocal student wishes to know is how to cause the vocal cords to assume the correct position for each register. On this, the most important topic of mechanical Voice Culture, Vocal Science has shed no light whatever. A student may hear descriptions of the laryngeal action, and study the highly interesting laryngoscopic photographs of the vocal cords, until thoroughly familiar with the theoretical side of the subject. Even then, the student is no better able to control the vocal cord action than when profoundly ignorant of the whole matter.

This deficiency of Vocal Science is frankly recognized by one of the latest authoritative writers on the subject, Dr. Wesley Mills. On page 173 of his work just quoted, he advises students to hear the great singers, to note carefully the quality of tone which characterizes each register, and to imitate these qualities with their own voices. This advice may almost be described as revolutionary. Vocal theorists have always assumed that the correct action cannot be acquired by imitation. In this advice to rely on the imitative faculty for acquiring control of the laryngeal action, Dr. Mills abandons the basic principle of modern methods. Without exception, all instruction in singing is to-day based on the idea of mechanical tone-production. An entirely new theory of Voice Culture is involved in this advice of Dr. Mills.

Turning to practical methods of instruction, it is found that the subject of registers is very seldom treated in the manner suggested by the theoretical works on the voice. This would be, to make the "placing" of the voice in the different registers the exclusive subject of instruction for a certain number of lessons;--to train each register of the voice separately;--when the correct vocal cord action had been established in each register, to unite the different registers, and to correct any "breaks" which might have developed. Comparatively few teachers attempt to follow this course. The great majority treat the registers in a much less systematic fashion. A single half-hour lesson usually includes explanations and exercises on several topics of mechanical tone-production, as well as hints on agility, style, execution, etc. As merely one of this variety of subjects, the registers usually receive rather desultory attention.

Some teachers profess to ignore the subject of registers entirely. They maintain that, when properly trained from the beginning, the compass of the voice is one homogeneous whole; "breaks" and changes of quality are in their opinion merely the results of bad instruction. But the general belief of vocal authorities is overwhelmingly against these teachers. The condition which they describe is without doubt the ideal of vocal management; but the vast majority of teachers believe that this condition cannot be attained without some attention being paid to the individual registers.

Most teachers recognize either two registers,--chest and head; or three,-- chest, middle, and head. Comparatively few extremists recognize more than three. Several sets of names for the registers have been proposed by vocal theorists,--thick and thin, long reed and short reed, high and low, etc. But these names have not been adopted by teachers to any extent.

One important phase of the registers has not received much attention from the laryngoscopic investigators. This is, that most of the notes of the voice's compass can be produced at will in more than one register. Vocal teachers as a rule recognize this fact. Julius Stockhausen for instance, in his

Gesangsmethode (Leipzig, 1884), says: "The registers cross each other. The two principal registers of the voice have many tones in common. The perfect blending of the registers on a single tone leads to the crescendo, called in Italian the messa di voce." Teachers generally do not set hard and fast limits to the extent of each register; they direct that in singing up the scale the student pass gradually from chest to middle, middle to head voice, etc.

In most practical methods the chest register occupies about the same position; this is also true of the head register. Even those teachers who profess to ignore registers recognize these two distinct qualities of tone; they instruct their pupils to sing low notes in one quality, and high notes in the other. This is in fact the general practice. In this connection the topics of registers and resonance are often combined. The terms "head voice," "head register," and "nasal resonance," are used interchangeably by the great majority of teachers. This is also true of the expressions "chest voice," "chest resonance," and "chest register."

In practical instruction, the extending of the compass of the voice is usually treated, rather loosely perhaps in most cases, as a feature of the registers. Methods vary greatly in points of detail, but in most of them instruction on this topic is given along the same general lines. Usually the three classes of voices receive different treatment, one form of instruction being used for sopranos and tenors, another for mezzo-sopranos and baritones, and a third for altos and bassos.

In teaching students with high voices, teachers usually "place"[5] the medium notes first, roughly speaking, from G to d (for male voices one octave lower). Then the lower notes are developed, mostly by descending scale passages, the lowest note practised being usually C. The high notes are sometimes "placed" by ascending scale passages and arpeggios, but more often by the octave jump and descending scale. There is room for considerable variation in this class of exercises, but they all conform to the same general principle.

[Note 5: The expression "placing the voice" is more fully treated in Chap. VI. It is assumed, however, that the reader is familiar with the ordinary usage of this expression.]

For mezzos and baritones about the same system is followed, the exercises being sung a major third or so lower. In the case of contraltos and bassos, the voice is usually trained from the middle in both directions. Most teachers favor the "chest voice" for singers of these types throughout the entire compass.

A discussion of the use of special vowels and consonants in this class of exercises is contained in Chapter V.

It must not be understood that this topic of instruction is assigned by many teachers to any particular period of the student's progress. Moreover, practice in the registers seldom forms the exclusive material of lessons and home study for any definite time. The wide range of topics considered in the average singing lesson has already been mentioned.

Very little connection can be traced between the scientific doctrine of registers, and the treatment which this subject receives in modern methods. This is only to be expected, in view of the fact that laryngoscopic investigation has not resulted in practical rules for managing the vocal cords. The registers of the voice are handled by modern teachers in a purely empirical fashion.

Movements of the Larynx, Tongue, and Soft Palate

It was remarked, in speaking of the registers, that no mechanical means has ever been found for directly controlling the operations of the vocal cords. To this statement one apparent exception is seen in the method originated by John Howard. This earnest student of the voice sought to carry out, to its logical conclusion, the accepted idea of mechanical vocal control. In this respect he stands practically alone. His is the only method which even pretends to reduce the entire operation of correct tone-production to a set of defined muscular contractions.

Howard's theories, with the details of a practical method based thereon, are fully described in his most important published work, The Physiology of Artistic Singing, New York, 1886. A complete exposition of Howard's theories is not called for here. For the present purpose the following short summary will suffice:

"The difference between correct tone-production and any incorrect vocal action is solely a matter of laryngeal adjustment and vocal cord action. Whether the tone produced be right or wrong, the influence of the resonance cavities is about the same. It is therefore idle to pay any attention to the subject of air resonance. Only one form of resonance is of any value in tone-production (considered as distinct from vowel formation). This is the sounding-board resonance of the bones of the head and chest. To secure this, the most important reinforcement of the tone, the larynx must be firmly held in a fixed position against the backbone, at the fifth cervical vertebra. All theories as to the registers of the voice, derived from laryngoscopic observation, are completely erroneous.

"In the production of tone, the muscular tissue of the vocal cords is thrown into vibration by the air blast, and not merely the membranous covering of the inner edges of the cords. For a soft tone, only a portion of the fleshy mass of the vocal cords vibrates; if this tone is gradually swelled to fortissimo, a constantly increasing portion of the muscular tissue is called into play. For the loudest tone, the entire mass of the vocal cords is bought into vibration. Thus the increased volume of the tone results not alone from the increase in the power of the breath blast. Each addition to the power of the expiration demands also a change in the adjustment of the vocal cords.

"The contractions of the muscles inside the larynx, including the vocal cords, cannot be brought under direct voluntary control. But these contractions can be regulated by the actions of other sets of muscles, viz., those by which the larynx is connected with the skeletal framework of the head, neck, and chest. These latter muscles can all be controlled by direct volition. Each of these sets of muscles has its function in tone-production. One set pulls the larynx backward, into the position already described, against the backbone. Two other opposed sets hold the larynx firmly in this position, one set pulling upward, the other downward. Finally, and most important in their influence on the actions of the vocal cords, a fourth set of muscles comes into play. These tilt the thyroid cartilage forward or backward, and thus bring about a greater or less tension of the vocal cords, independent of the contractions of the muscles of the vocal cords themselves. In this way is regulated the amount of the fleshy mass of the vocal cords exposed to the expiratory blast. Correct tone-production results when exactly the necessary degree of strength is exerted by each one of these four sets of muscles."

For each of these groups of muscles Howard devised a system of exercises and drills by which the singer is supposed to bring all the movements involved under direct voluntary control. The parts thus exercised are the tongue, the soft palate, the jaw, the fauces, and also the muscles by which the larynx is raised and lowered in the throat, and those by which the chest is raised. In teaching a pupil Howard took up each part in turn. A sufficient number of lessons was devoted to each set of muscles for the pupil (presumably) to acquire the necessary control of each group.

Howard also paid much attention to the breath; he worked out the system of high-chest breathing in a really masterly fashion. But his manner of dealing with this subject did not differ from that of a great number of other teachers.

Howard retired from active teaching about 1895. His theories of the vocal action have never been generally accepted by vocal theorists, and the number of teachers who now profess to follow his method is very small. There are, however, many other masters whose methods, in their main features, are patterned after Howard's. These latter teachers may therefore be justly said to follow the Howard system, even though they give him no credit for their doctrines of vocal control.

Howard usually insisted that his pupils should understand the theoretical basis of his method, and the exact purpose of each exercise and muscular contraction. But as a rule his successors do not make this demand on their pupils. They are content to have the students practise the prescribed exercises; this the students do, with very little thought about the theory lying behind the method. For the pupil this system, as at present generally taught, consists solely of a series of muscular drills for the tongue, larynx, palate, etc.

In this review of modern methods, the Howard system is important, mainly because it represents the consistent application of the idea of mechanical tone-production. As was observed, Howard's theories had very little influence on the general trend of Vocal Science. The external features of the Howard system are indeed shared to some extent by the methods of many other teachers. Muscular drills of about the same type are very widely used. Some teachers go so far in this respect that their methods might almost be confounded with the Howard system. But the resemblance is purely external.

Even in 1880, at the time when Howard had fairly perfected his method, there was nothing novel about exercises of this type. The first attempts at a practical study of vocal mechanics consisted of observations of those parts of the vocal organs whose movements can be readily seen and felt. These are the lips, tongue, palate, and larynx. Garcia's Memoire, already cited, is mainly a record of observations of this kind. Nearly every vocal theorist since that time has also paid some attention to this phase of the vocal action.

In practical methods of instruction, elaborate systems of rules have long been in use for governing the positions of the tongue, lips, palate, etc. Unlike the Howard theory, no definite scientific basis is usually given for specific directions of this kind. Each investigator has simply noted how certain great singers held their tongues or soft palates, whether the larynx was held high or low in the throat, etc., and considered that these must be the correct positions. It would be hard to find a greater diversity of opinion on any topic connected with the voice than is encountered here. To enumerate all the rules which are given for governing the actions of each part would be useless. A few of the contradictory opinions regarding the correct position of the larynx will suffice to show how great is the confusion on this topic:

"The larynx should be held low in the throat for all tones." "It should be held in a fixed position high in the throat." "It should be high for low tones, and should descend as the pitch rises." "It should be in a low position for the lowest note of each register, and should rise as the pitch rises; when the highest note of the register is reached, it should at once descend for the lowest note of the next register." Prominent teachers and writers could be cited as authority for each of these rules, and indeed for several others. A similar diversity of opinion is found regarding the rules given for the position of the tongue and the soft palate.

Practices vary greatly as to the amount of time and attention devoted to muscular drills of the parts under consideration, and also as to the importance attached to the positions of these parts. Some teachers make this a prominent feature of their methods. The majority, however, treat the subject much more lightly. They now and then devote a part of the lesson time to the muscular drills and exercises; for the rest, an occasional hint or correction regarding the positions of the parts is deemed sufficient.

All the movements of the tongue, lips, and jaw are directly under voluntary control. Exercises for these parts are therefore given only for acquiring suppleness and agility. The muscular movements of the larynx and soft palate are readily brought under control. Each can simply be raised and lowered. A few minutes' daily practice, extended over three or four weeks, is generally sufficient for the student to acquire satisfactory command of these actions. But to hold the tongue, palate, and larynx in any prescribed position, while singing a tone, is an extremely troublesome matter. Those teachers who adhere to precise systems for the positions of these parts, frequently impose much arduous practice on their pupils. As to the merits of any special system of the kind, this question is reserved for future discussion.

Attack

It would be hard to determine when the term "attack" was first used to describe the starting of a vocal tone. Nor is it easy to define the precise position assigned to the subject of attack by vocal theorists. No satisfactory statement of the theory of attack can be cited from any published treatise on Vocal Science. It is commonly asserted, rather loosely indeed, that the tone must be "started right." As Clara Kathleen Rogers expresses it, "Attack the tone badly, and nothing can improve it afterwards." (The Philosophy of Singing, New York, 1893.) This statement is in the practical sense utterly unfounded. A tone may be "attacked" with a nasal or throaty quality, and then be improved, by simply eliminating the objectionable quality. Of this fact the reader may readily convince himself. In short, all the accepted theories of attack rest on an unscientific basis.

Vocal theorists generally treat the subject of attack as connected in some way with registers and laryngeal action. But as no rule has ever been formulated for the mechanical management of the laryngeal action, it necessarily follows that no intelligible directions are ever given to the student for preparing to start the laryngeal action correctly.

Three possible ways of attacking a tone are generally recognized. These are described by Albert B. Bach, in The Principles of Singing, second edition, London, 1897. They are, first, the stroke of the glottis. (This is advocated by Garcia in most of his published works, although the testimony of many of his pupils, notably Mme. Marchesi, is that Garcia used the glottic stroke very little in actual instruction.) Second, the aspirate (h as in have), which is generally condemned. Third, the approximation of the vocal cords at the precise instant the breath blast strikes them. This latter mode of attack is advocated by Browne and Behnke, who call it the "slide of the glottis." It must be observed that neither the stroke nor the slide of the glottis can be shown to have any influence in causing the laryngeal muscles to adopt any particular mode of adjustment.

Turning to practical methods of instruction, little connection can be traced between the theories of attack and the occasional directions usually given for starting the tone. The subject of attack is seldom assigned to any particular period in the course of study. Many teachers ignore the matter altogether. Others devote a few minutes now and then to drilling a pupil in the stroke of the glottis, without attaching much importance to the subject. (The position assigned to this mode of attack by the "breath-band" theorists has already been mentioned.) On the whole, the matter of attack is usually treated rather loosely. The pupil is occasionally interrupted in singing a phrase, and told to "attack the tone better." Needless to say, this form of instruction is in no sense scientific.

CHAPTER IV

RESONANCE

In order to understand fully the position in Vocal Science assigned to the doctrine of resonance, it is necessary to trace the origin and the development of this doctrine. The old Italian masters naturally knew nothing whatever of resonance, nor of any other topic of acoustics. Yet the accepted theories of resonance in its relation to the voice are directly based on a set of empirical observations made by the old masters. The facts which they noted are now a matter of common knowledge. In singing low notes a sensation of trembling or vibration is felt in the upper chest; high notes are accompanied by a similar sensation in the head. How these sensations of vibration came to be made the basis of the theories of vocal resonance, and of registers as well, is an interesting bit of vocal history.

Although almost entirely ignorant of vocal mechanics in the scientific sense, the old masters were eager students of the voice. They carefully noted the characteristic sound of each tone of the voice, and worked out what they believed to be a comprehensive theory of tone-production. One of their observations was that in every voice the low notes have a somewhat different quality from the high notes. To distinguish these two qualities of tone the old masters adopted the word used for a similar purpose by the organ builders,--register. Further, they noted the sensation of vibration in the chest caused by singing low notes, and concluded that these notes are actually produced in the chest. To the lower notes of the voice they therefore gave the name "chest register." As Tosi explains it, "Voce di Petto is a full voice, which comes from the breast by strength." For a precisely similar reason, viz., the sensation of vibration in the head felt in singing the higher notes, this portion of the voice was called by the old masters the "head register."

When the study of vocal mechanics along scientific lines was undertaken, in the early decades of the nineteenth century, attention was at first paid almost exclusively to the subject of registers. The questions then most discussed were the number of registers, the number of notes which each should include, and the precise point of production of each register in the chest, throat, and head. Garcia's Memoire, dealing with the registers, was noticed in the preceding chapter. He showed that different adjustments of the tongue, palate, and larynx are concerned in the production of the various registers. This Memoire opened up a new line of observation, in which Garcia continued to take the lead. But the extending of the scope of inquiry concerning the registers did not result in any unanimity of opinion on the part of the vocal investigators of that time.

For a few years following the invention of the laryngoscope (1855), vocal theorists ceased their disputes about the registers, and awaited the definite results of this new mode of observation. When this potent little instrument was put within the reach of every investigator, it was believed that the mystery surrounding the registers was about to be dispelled.

One important consequence of the invention of the laryngoscope was the turning of attention away from the sensations of vibration in the chest and head. Each register was ascribed to a distinct mode of operation of the vocal cords, and for several years the terms "chest voice" and "head voice" were held to be scientifically unsound. But with the publication of Helmholtz's Die

Lehre von den Tonempfindungen in 1863, the sensations of vibration again received attention. These sensations were then made the basis of a theory of vocal resonance, which has since been adopted by the great majority of vocal scientists.

Until the publication of Helmholtz's work vocal theorists had known practically nothing of acoustics. The fact that the tones produced by the vocal cords are increased in power and modified in quality by the resonance of the air in the mouth-pharynx cavity came as a distinct revelation to the theoretical students of the voice. Helmholtz confined his experiments and demonstrations to the mouth-pharynx cavity, and investigated in particular the influence of this cavity in producing the various vowel and consonant sounds. But vocal theorists at once extended the idea of air resonance, and connected it with the well-known sensations of vibration in the chest and head. It was assumed that these sensations are caused by vibrations of the air in the chest and nasal cavities.

This assumption has been accepted without question by the great majority of vocal scientists. Both the chest voice and the head voice are now believed to owe their distinctive qualities to the reinforcing vibrations of the air in the chest and nasal cavities respectively. The mere fact that these vibrations can be felt is held sufficient proof of the statement. "In every true chest tone the resonance can be distinctly felt as a vibration (fremitus pectoralis) by the hand laid flat on the chest." (Die Kunst der idealen Tonbildung, Dr. W. Reinecke, Leipzig, 1906.) It must be observed that this is by no means a satisfactory scientific proof of the doctrine of chest resonance. This feature of the subject is reserved for discussion later.

The doctrine of resonance is now generally accepted as one of the basic principles of Vocal Science. It is stated, in substance, by almost every authority on the voice that "The tone produced by the vibration of the vocal cords, even when the laryngeal action is correct in every way, is weak, of poor quality, and without character. This tone must be strengthened and made of musical quality by utilizing the influence of resonance." The subject of resonance is always treated in theoretical works on the voice under the three heads of chest, mouth-pharynx, and nasal resonance. To these a fourth is sometimes added,--the sounding-board resonance of the bones of the chest and head.

Mouth-Pharynx Resonance

Considered strictly in its bearing on tone-production, the resonance of the mouth-pharynx cavity does not receive much attention from theoretical observers of the voice. The form assumed by this cavity is of necessity determined by the vowel to be sung. Aside from its function in the pronunciation of words, the influence of mouth-pharynx resonance on the tones of the voice is seldom discussed by vocal scientists.

As a rule, vocal teachers pay little attention to this form of resonance. The subject of enunciation is generally treated as distinct from tone-production strictly speaking. While the correct emission of the tone, in its passage from the vocal cords to the lips, is considered a very important topic, this feature of tone-production has no reference to resonance.

One exception must be made to the statement that no attention is paid to mouth-pharynx resonance. This is found in an interpretation of the empirical precept, "Sing with open throat." Several vocal theorists take this precept literally, and hold that it describes a function of mouth-pharynx resonance. According to their idea the cavity must be expanded to the largest size possible, on the theory that a large resonance cavity secures a proportionately greater reinforcement of the tone. "The greater the size of the pharynx, whether through practice or natural gifts, the stronger in proportion is the tone." (Die Kunst der idealen Tonbildung, Dr. W. Reinecke, Leipzig, 1906.) This theory is of course rather loose and unscientific. Still this idea,--a literal interpretation of the "open throat" precept,--receives much attention in practical instruction.

Only one muscular action has ever been defined by which the throat might be "opened." That is, the lowering of the larynx and the raising of the soft palate. Many teachers therefore direct that the throat be "opened" gradually in this way for the swelling of the tone. It is assumed that the power of the voice is developed by singing with the larynx low in the throat. This manner of instruction is, however, very loosely given. The supposedly scientific interpretation of the "open throat" precept shades off into a purely empirical application.

Chest Resonance

In no other topic of Vocal Science is the gap between theory and practice more striking than in the doctrine of chest resonance. Vocal teachers are in fair accord in believing the resonance of the air in the chest to be the most important influence in imparting power and "color" to the voice, and particularly to the lower notes of its compass. Students of singing are in almost all cases urged to acquire a proper command of chest resonance. But when it comes to telling the student how to learn to govern the chest resonance, the teacher has practically nothing to offer. No direct means has ever been found for causing the air in the thorax to vibrate; this cannot be effected, so far as has yet been determined, by any voluntary muscular action on the part of the singer.

This being the case, intelligible instruction in the use and management of chest resonance is hardly to be expected. Teachers of singing are obliged to fall back on purely empirical instruction on this topic. This usually takes the form of a description of the sensations experienced by the singer when producing tones in the chest voice. How this description of the singer's sensations is applied, is discussed in the following chapter.

Nasal Resonance

The lack of connection between the theories of vocal scientists and the practical methods of singing teachers is well illustrated in the subject of nasal resonance. A striking feature of all the discussions concerning the use or avoidance of nasal resonance is the fact that vocal theorists base their opinions entirely on empirical observations. The use of nasal resonance is condemned by almost every prominent authority on Vocal Science. Yet the only reason ever advanced for condemning nasal resonance is the fact that a tone of objectionable nasal quality seems to "come through the nose." This fact cannot, of course, be questioned. It is mentioned by Tosi, who speaks of the "defect of singing through the nose," and is observed by everybody possessed of an ear keen enough to detect the nasal quality of sound.

It is generally stated by vocal theorists that the nasal quality is imparted to the tone by the influence of the resonance of the air in the nasal cavities. In order to prove this assertion Browne and Behnke offer the following experiment, (quoted in substance): "Hold a hand-mirror flat, face up, just below the nostrils. Then sing a nasal tone; you will note that the mirror is clouded, showing that part of the breath has passed through the nasal cavities. Now sing another tone, free from the fault of nasal quality; this time the mirror is not clouded, which proves that no air has passed through the cavities in question." (Voice, Song and Speech.) This experiment is simplified by other authorities, who direct that the nostrils be pinched by the fingers, and then allowed to open by the removal of the pressure of the fingers. A steady tone is meanwhile to be sung. It will be noted, according to these theorists, that with the nostrils open the tone is nasal, and with the nostrils closed the tone is not nasal. This proves to their satisfaction that a tone passing in whole or in part through the nasal cavities must be nasal in quality.

It must be noted here that these experiments are not in any sense convincing. A tone of objectionable nasal quality can be sung equally well with the nostrils either closed or open, and so can a tone free from the nasal quality.

In theory, the mechanical prevention of nasal resonance is very simple. It is necessary only to raise the soft palate in singing, and thus to cut off the expired breath from passing into the nasal cavities. Most vocal scientists advise that the singer hold the soft palate raised for every tone.

Practical teachers of singing pay little attention to the theoretical discussions concerning nasal resonance. The overwhelming majority of teachers are firm believers in nasal resonance, and make it an important feature of their methods. They believe that this resonance is the most important factor in giving to the tone its "point," brilliance, and carrying power.

So far as instruction in the use of nasal resonance is concerned, teachers owe but little to the mechanical doctrines of Vocal Science. No voluntary muscular operation has ever been found, by which the air in the nasal cavities can be directly thrown into vibration, and so made to reinforce the tones of the voice. Instruction in the management of nasal resonance is therefore similar to that in chest resonance. The teacher describes the sensations experienced by a singer who produces the exact quality of tone desired. Use is also made of special vowels and consonants, for (supposedly) acquiring command of nasal resonance. A description of this form of instruction is given in the following chapter.

Sounding-Board Resonance

The acoustic principle of sounding-board resonance, in its application to the voice, is discussed by several vocal scientists. It is usually treated under two heads: first, the entire body is looked upon as a sounding board, capable of reinforcing the tones of the voice under certain conditions. Second, the bones of the chest and of the head are thought to be thrown into vibration, in sympathy with the vibrations of the air in the chest and nasal cavities respectively.

The importance attached by Howard to the sounding-board resonance of the entire body has already been noticed. Aside from the teachers of the Howard system, very few masters pay any attention to this feature of vocal reinforcement. Those who do so have no difficulty in dealing with the subject. When the singer stands in the position generally considered correct for singing, the body is said to be in the position most favorable for securing the benefits of this form of resonance. For this no special rules or exercises are needed.

Very little attention is paid, in practical instruction, to the vibrations of the bones of the resonance cavities. Each cavity is treated as a whole; the fact is only occasionally mentioned that the bones inclosing the cavities may vibrate, as well as the inclosed air.

CHAPTER V

EMPIRICAL MATERIALS OF MODERN METHODS

A series of topics included in modern methods is now to be considered, different in scope from the strictly mechanical features of tone-production so far described. It must be apparent to the reader that the present understanding of the muscular processes of singing is not sufficient to furnish a complete method of instruction. This fact is thoroughly appreciated by the teachers of singing. Almost without exception they seek to supplement the mechanical doctrines by instruction of an entirely different character. The subjects included in this form of instruction are of several classes. They comprise the manner of emission of the tone, the traditional precepts of the old Italian school, the singer's sensations, and the use of certain vowels and consonants for special purposes.

Emission and Forward Placing

Of all the traditional precepts, the one most frequently cited in theoretical treatises on the voice is, "Place the tone forward." For this precept it is generally believed that a satisfactory explanation has been found in the accepted doctrine of tone emission.

The characteristic effect of perfect singing known as the "forward tone" is thoroughly well known to every lover of singing. In some peculiar way the tone, when perfectly produced, seems to issue directly from the singer's mouth. When we listen to a poorly trained and faulty singer the tones seem to be caught somewhere in the singer's throat. We feel instinctively that if the singer could only lift the voice off the throat, and bring it forward in the mouth, the tones would be greatly improved in character. It is commonly believed that the old masters knew some way in which this can be done. Just what means they used for this purpose is not known. But the accepted scientific interpretation of the "forward tone" precept is held by vocal theorists to render the subject perfectly clear.

Sir Morell Mackenzie states the correct emission of the tone as one of the three cardinal principles of the vocal action. "The regulation of the force of the blast which strikes against the vocal cords, the placing of these in the most favourable position for the effect which it is desired to produce, and the direction of the vibrating column of air which issues from the larynx are the three elements of artistic production." (The Hygiene of the Vocal Organs, London, 1886.) His analysis of the mechanical and acoustic processes involved in emission may be cited as typical of the views of the great majority of vocal scientists. "It (the column of sound) must be projected against the roof of the cavity behind the upper front teeth, from which it rebounds sharply and clearly to the outside." Mme. Seiler expresses the idea somewhat differently, but the meaning is about the same. "A correct disposition of the tones of the voice consists in causing the air, brought into vibration by the vocal ligaments, to rebound from immediately above the front teeth, where it must be concentrated as much as possible, rebounding thence to form in the mouth continuous vibrations." (The Voice in Singing, Phila., 1886.)

To the vocal theorists this is no doubt thoroughly convincing and satisfactory. But as a topic of practical instruction in singing this theory of tone emission is utterly valueless. How can the "column of vocalized breath" be voluntarily directed in its passage through the pharynx and mouth? No muscular process has ever been located, by which the singer can influence the course of the expired breath, and direct it to any specific point in the mouth. Even if the expired breath does, in perfect singing, take the course described, knowledge of this fact cannot enable the singer to bring this about. The accepted doctrine of tone emission is of no benefit whatever to the teacher of singing. He knows what the "forward tone" is, that is, what it sounds like, just as well no doubt as did the old Italian master. But if the latter knew how to enable his pupils to obtain the "forward" character of tone, the modern teacher is to that extent not so well off.

In view of the prevailing ignorance of any means for securing the (supposedly) correct emission of tone, intelligible instruction on this topic is hardly to be expected. But the great majority of teachers lay great stress on the need of acquiring the correct emission. The best they can do is to explain the scientific doctrine to their pupils; the students are generally left to find for themselves some way of applying the explanation. In many cases the master tries to assist the student by describing the singer's sensations, experienced when producing a "forward" tone.

Certain vowels and consonants are usually held to be especially favored by a "forward position," and exercises on these are very widely used for securing a "forward" tone. These exercises are described in a later paragraph. It will be noticed however that this use of vowels is not an application of the theory of "forward emission." The vowel sounds are believed to owe their "forward position" to resonance, while "emission" is purely a matter of direction or focusing of the breath-blast. The whole subject of emission and forward placing is in a very unsatisfactory condition.

The Traditional Precepts in Modern Instruction

So much importance is attached by modern teachers to the traditional precepts of the old school that this subject calls for somewhat lengthy treatment. Before discussing the manner in which the precepts are applied in practical instruction, it will be well to review first the interpretations of the precepts offered by different vocal scientists.

It must be remarked, in the first place, that no single one of the precepts has ever been satisfactorily explained; that is, no direct means of performing the actions indicated by the precepts has ever been found. If ever the precepts had a definite meaning, considered as specific directions for performing certain actions in a special way, that meaning has been lost. Mechanical analysis has not reduced the precepts to a form in which they are of direct value to the modern teacher.

That the "forward tone" is interpreted as a reference to the emission of the voice was noted earlier in this chapter. The explanation of the "open throat" precept as a function of mouth-pharynx resonance has also been mentioned.

"Singing on the breath" is a very perplexing subject for vocal theorists. Many authorities assert that this precept describes an effect obtained by the "opposed muscular action" breath-control. (See citation from Shakespeare in Chapter II.) But this explanation is hardly satisfactory; if the precept had meant no more than breath-control, it would have been forgotten long ago.

The "support of the tone" is mentioned by a large number of theoretical writers on the voice. These writers generally state, in substance, that "the tone must be supported by the breathing muscles of the chest, and not by the throat muscles." (See The Technics of Bel Canto, by G. B. Lamperti, New York, 1905.) But this explanation is hardly to be considered as a scientific doctrine. Every one knows that a tone has no weight, so in the physical sense it can need no support. In short, scientific analysis has thrown no more light on this than any other of the old precepts.

Notwithstanding the modern teacher's complete ignorance of the mechanical operations which they seem to indicate, the old precepts form a very important feature of instruction in singing. The great majority of teachers cite these precepts constantly, and frequently direct their pupils to "open the throat," to "bring the tone forward," etc. Is it to be believed that an intelligent master would use these directions in any occult or cabalistic sense?

Such a statement is occasionally made by a consistent upholder of the mechanical system of Voice Culture. Paulo Guetta, for example, in a recent exhaustive work on the subject, ridicules the use of the old precepts. Says this ardent advocate of mechanical instruction in singing:

"Nowadays alchemy and necromancy awaken nothing but curiosity. How then can one who thinks and reasons admit that an art can be cultivated and sustained by theories extravagant, fantastic, enigmatic, explained and condensed in abstruse phrases and sentences, which not only have no meaning whatever, but even lead one to doubt whether the teacher himself knows what result it is desired to obtain? Do you wish a little example? Behold!

"'Press the whole voice against the mask.' 'Place the voice in the head.' 'The voice is directed to the nasal cavities.' 'Place the voice forward.'

"Others, with the most austere gravity, will tell you that your voice is too far back, or that you send the voice to the lower teeth, and promise in a few days to place the voice forward, at the upper teeth, or wherever else it should be." (Il Canto nel suo Mecanismo, Milan, 1902.)

This statement is by no means justified. The precepts have a real and definite meaning for the vocal teacher. Any one familiar with the highest type of artistic singing must have observed that the singer's "throat seems to be open"; the tones impress the hearer as being in some way "forward in the singer's mouth," and not at the vocal cords; the voice "seems to be supported" somewhere; the tones float out freely on the breath. A harsh and badly produced voice seems to be held in the singer's throat by main force. The critical hearer feels instinctively that such a singer's voice would be greatly improved if the tones could only be supported in a forward position in the mouth, and kept from slipping back into the throat. It seems that this would relieve the throat of the strain of holding the tone; the throat would then be open, and the voice would float out freely on the breath.

In short, the traditional precepts describe accurately the most striking points of difference between perfect singing and bad singing, so far as the effect on the listener is concerned. Modern teachers are thoroughly familiar with the highest standards of the vocal art; they fully appreciate how well the precepts describe the perfection of singing. Through long continued listening to voices, the precepts come to have a very real meaning. It is inevitable therefore that the teacher should try to impart to the pupil this intimate feeling for the voice. True, this acquaintance with the voice is purely empirical; as has just been remarked, no mechanical analysis of this empirical knowledge has ever been successfully made. The modern teacher's apprehension of the meaning of the precepts is only very vaguely connected with a supposed insight into the mechanical processes of tone-production.

Yet there is nothing vague about the impression made on the teacher in listening to his pupils. On the contrary, every faulty tone impresses the teacher very keenly and definitely as being too far back, or as caught in the throat, or as falling back for lack of support, etc. How could it be expected then, that the teacher should refrain from telling the pupil to correct the faulty production, in the manner so clearly and directly indicated by the tones?

But this direct application of the precepts is of absolutely no value in instruction, because of the teacher's ignorance of the mechanical processes supposedly involved. There is after all some justification for Guetta's criticism of empirical instruction. It is all very well for the teacher to feel that the pupil's voice is gripped in the throat, and to bid him "open your throat." The pupil may strive ever so earnestly to open his throat, but he does not know how, and the teacher is utterly unable to tell him.

All instruction based on the empirical precepts is thus seen to be extremely unsatisfactory. While the precepts convey a very valuable meaning to the teacher, no way has ever been found for translating this meaning into rules for the mechanical management of the vocal organs. Recourse is had, to some extent, to a description of the singer's sensations; exercises on special vowels and consonants are also much used, for imparting the ideas embodied in the precepts. Both of these topics are now to be considered.

The Singer's Sensations

The correct use of the voice awakens in the singer a variety of sensations generally held to be different from those accompanying any incorrect vocal action.

One important fact must first be noted regarding the manner in which the singer's sensations are described by various authorities. The use of the voice awakens a wide variety of local sensations, which bear no necessary relation to each other. A singer may, at will, pay entire attention to any one, or to any particular set, of these sensations, and for the time being completely ignore all the others.

Physiologically considered, the singer's sensations are of two classes,--first, muscular sensations strictly speaking; and second, a sense of tingling or vibration, definitely located usually about the breast bone, and in the front and upper part of the head.

Muscular Sensations of Singing

It is very difficult to analyze and describe exactly the muscular sensations which accompany any complex action. Swimming, diving, dancing, skating,-- each awakens a set of extremely vivid muscular feelings; yet to describe these sensations so graphically that they could be felt in imagination by one who had never experienced them actually,--that would be almost impossible.

This peculiar aspect of muscular sensations is particularly true as regards the action of singing. While every vocal teacher knows exactly how it feels to sing properly, all descriptions of the singer's muscular sensations are extremely vague. But the vividness of these sensations keeps them constantly before the teacher's mind, and some application of them, in the present state of Voice Culture, is almost inevitable.

The basic sensation of correct singing, as generally described, is a feeling of perfect poise and harmony of the whole body; this is accompanied by a sense of freedom about the throat and jaw, and firm grasp and control of the expiratory muscles. Attempts are frequently made to amplify this description, but the results are always very vague. A feeling of "absence of local effort" at the throat is much spoken of, or "perfect relaxation of the vocal muscles."

A few specially localized muscular sensations are also much discussed. Descriptions of this class however are often so loosely given as to render a definite statement almost impossible. Most frequently mentioned are the feeling of "backward pressure in the throat," and of "drinking in the tone," instead of sending it out. Then again, the "tone must be felt at the upper front teeth." A feeling as of an "expanded and flexible vocal tube, extending from the base of the lungs to the lips," is also much talked of. "Feel that you grow bigger as the tone swells" is about as intelligible as the feeling of "floating jaw."

On the whole, the subject of the singer's muscular sensations is usually rather mystifying to the student.

Sensations of Tingling or Vibration

Descriptions of sensations of this class are much more coherent than those just considered. A definite location is given to the feelings, in the chest and in the head.

A feeling of trembling in the upper chest is usually held to indicate that the chest cavity is working properly as a resonator. This sensation is therefore the chief reliance of most teachers in "placing" the lower tones, especially for low voices. Sensations in the nasal cavities and head are utilized for acquiring control of nasal resonance, for placing the upper notes of the voice, and for "bringing the voice forward." Exercises for control of both cavities, on special vowels and consonants, combine the two topics, "vowel position" and sensation.

Singing in the Mask

In recent years a method of instruction has been developed in France, which is commonly called by its advocates "singing in the mask." The basic idea of this method is that the singer must imagine his face to be covered by a mask, and must "sing into this mask." This idea may seem rather vague at first; but a few trials will show how easy it is for the singer to persuade himself that he projects his voice into his face.

This method goes to the extreme in utilizing the sensations of vibration in the nose and forehead. These sensations are analyzed, localized, and described, down to the most minute detail. While other topics of instruction are included,--breathing, registers, position of tongue, larynx, palate, etc., everything else is subordinated to nasal resonance. "Singing in the mask" is of course a purely empirical method, and little has been attempted in the way of justifying it on scientific principles.

* * *

All instruction based on the singer's sensations is purely empirical, in the meaning ordinarily attached to this word in treatises on Vocal Science. Theoretical works on the voice seldom touch on the subject of sensations, nor do the vocal teachers generally make this subject prominent when speaking of their methods.[6]

[Note 6: An exception to this statement is seen in the recently published book of Mme. Lilli Lehmann, Meine Gesangskunst, Berlin, 1902. This famous artist and teacher devotes by far the greater part of her book to a minute analysis and description of the singer's sensations.]

Sensations occupy a rather peculiar position in modern methods. They are a distinctly subsidiary element of instruction and are seldom raised to the dignity accorded to the mechanical doctrines of vocal management. The use of the singer's sensations, as applied in practical instruction, is almost exclusively interpretive. In the mechanical sense the traditional precepts have no meaning whatever; this is also true of several of the accepted doctrines of Vocal Science. For example, the precept "Support the tone," is absolutely meaningless as a principle of mechanical vocal action. But, when interpreted as referring to a set of sensations experienced by the singer, this precept takes on a very definite meaning. Nobody knows what the support of the tone is, but every vocal teacher knows how it feels. In the same way, no means is known for directly throwing the air in the nasal cavities into vibration. But the sensation in the front of the head, which indicates, presumably, the proper action of nasal resonance, is familiar to all teachers. Most of the positive materials of modern methods are thus interpreted in terms of sensations.

True, the accepted theory of Vocal Science does not directly countenance this interpretation. The basic principle of modern Voice Culture is the idea of mechanical vocal management. All instruction is supposed to aim at direct, conscious, and voluntary control of the muscular operations of singing. Teachers always impart to their pupils this idea of the mechanical control of the voice. The vocal action is always considered from the mechanical side. Even those expressions whose mechanical meaning is vague or unscientific are yet used as referring definitely to muscular actions. The conscious thought of the teacher is always turned to the mechanical idea supposedly conveyed by scientific doctrine and empirical precept. The translation of this idea into a description of sensations is almost always the result of a sub-conscious mental process.

It therefore follows that in practical instruction the appeal to sensations is more often indirect than direct. For example, when a student's tones are caught in the throat, the master says explicitly,--"Free the tone by opening your throat." The master explains the (supposed) wrong vocal action, and describes how the tone should be produced. Incidentally, the master may also tell how and where the tone should be felt.

There is also a great deal of instruction based frankly and directly on the singer's sensations. Instruction of this type usually takes the form of special exercises on certain vowels and consonants, which are believed to be peculiarly suited for imparting command of particular features of the correct vocal action. The topics generally covered are chest resonance, nasal resonance, open throat, and forward placing of the tone. This form of instruction is held to be referable in some way to scientific principles. The laws of vowel and consonant formation formulated by Helmholtz are often cited in proof of the efficacy of exercises of this type. There is also much discussion of the "location" of the tone. But there is little justification for the statement that instruction based on the singer's sensations is scientific in character. A misconception of acoustic principles is evidenced by most of the statements made concerning the use of special vowels and consonants in securing the correct vocal action. The exercises which aim to utilize the singer's sensations in producing particular vowels and consonants are now to be described.

Exercises on Special Vowels and Consonants

Of the rules concerning the use of special vowels, probably the most important is that a (as in far) is the most favorable vowel for the general purposes of voice training. Teachers generally have their pupils sing most of their exercises on this vowel. Much attention is paid to the exact pronunciation of the vowel, and fine distinctions are drawn between its various sounds in Italian, French, German, and English. The preference for the Italian pronunciation is very general. It is claimed for this sound that it helps materially in acquiring command of the "open throat." Indeed, a peculiar virtue in this regard is ascribed to the Italian vowels generally. No convincing reason has ever been given for this belief. But the usual custom is to "place the voice" on the Italian a, and then to take up, one at a time, the other Italian vowels.

The labial consonants, p, b, t, d, are believed to have a peculiar influence in securing the "forward position" of the tone. Much the same influence is also ascribed to the vowel oo, although many authorities consider i (Italian) the "most forward" vowel. Exercises combining these consonants and vowels are very widely used, on single tones, and on groups of three, four, or five notes. The syllables boo, poo, too, doo are practised, or if the teacher hold to the other "forward" vowel, bee, pee, tee, dee; the student is instructed to hold the vowel in the "forward position" secured by the initial consonant. Later on, the "forward" vowel is gradually widened into the other vowels; exercises are sung on boo-ah, doo-ah, etc. This form of instruction is capable of great elaboration. Many teachers use a wide variety of combinations of these vowels and consonants; but as the basic idea is always the same, this class of exercises calls for no further description. The singer's sensations, notably those of "open throat," "expanded vocal tube," "forward tone," and vibration in the chest, are generally brought to the pupil's attention in this form of exercise.

Another set of sounds are held to be specially adapted for securing the use of nasal resonance. These are the letters m, n, and ng, when used for starting a tone, and also the vowel i (Italian). The exercises used are similar in character to those just described. In singing these exercises, the student is supposed to "start the tone high up in the head on the initial m or n, and to hold it there, while gradually and smoothly opening the mouth for the vowel," etc. The sensations specially noticed in this type of exercise are the feelings of vibration in the nose and forehead. The "forward tone," as well as the nasal resonance, is supposed to be favored by the practice of these exercises.

Enunciation

Vocal teachers always recognize the importance of a clear delivery of the text in singing. Correct enunciation is therefore considered in all methods. A few teachers believe that a clear pronunciation helps greatly to establish the correct vocal action. Some even go so far as to say that a clear delivery of the words will of itself insure a correct tone-production. But this theory calls for only passing comment. One has but to turn to the vaudeville stage to see its falsity. For singers of that class, the words are of the utmost importance, while the tone-production is usually of the very worst.

A few teachers base their methods on the theory that correct tone-production results necessarily from the singing of "pure vowels." This is no doubt interesting, but still far from convincing. The problem of tone-production is not solved quite so simply.

As a rule, vocal teachers consider the subject of pronunciation as quite distinct from tone-production. Methods differ with regard to the use of exercises in articulation, and to the stage of progress at which these exercises are taken up. Some teachers insist on their pupils practising singing for months on the vowels, before permitting them to sing even the simplest songs with words. Others have the pupils sing words from the beginning of instruction. As a rule, teachers begin to give songs, and vocalises with words, very early in the course.

Throat Stiffness and Relaxing Exercises

Teachers of singing generally recognize that any stiffening of the throat interferes with the correct action of the voice. Yet for some strange reason vocal students are very much inclined to form habits of throat stiffness. This constantly happens, in spite of the fact that teachers continually warn their pupils against the tendency to stiffen. On this account, exercises for relaxing the throat are an important feature of modern instruction in singing.

Naturally, relaxing exercises are not thought to have any direct bearing in bringing about the correct vocal action. They are purely preparatory; their purpose is only to bring the vocal organs into the right condition for constructive training. For this reason, the means used for relaxing the throat are seldom mentioned among the materials of instruction. But almost every vocal teacher is obliged to make frequent use of throat relaxing exercises. Indeed, throat stiffness is one of the most serious difficulties of modern Voice Culture. A student frequently seems to be making good progress, and then without much warning falls into a condition of throat stiffness so serious as to undo for a time the good work of several months' study. In such a case there is nothing for the teacher to do but to drop the progressive work, and devote a few lessons to relaxing exercises.

Little difficulty is usually found in relaxing the throat, when once the necessity becomes strikingly apparent. That is, provided progressive study is dropped for a time, and attention paid solely to relaxing exercises. But such cases are comparatively rare. A much more constant source of trouble is found in the prevailing tendency of vocal students to stiffen their throats, just enough to interfere with the (supposed) application of the teacher's method.

The exercises used for relaxing the throat are fairly simple, both in character and scope. They consist mainly of toneless yawning, of single tones "yawned out" on a free exhalation, and of descending scale passages of the same type. Although seldom recognized as a coordinate topic of instruction, exercises of this character are usually interspersed among the other materials of vocal methods.

CHAPTER VI

A GENERAL VIEW OF MODERN VOICE CULTURE

All the materials of modern methods have now been described. The subject next to be considered is the manner in which these materials are utilized in practical instruction. In other words, what is a method of Voice Culture?

In the present state of Vocal Science, the subject of tone-production overshadows everything else in difficulty. When once the correct vocal action has been acquired, the student's progress is assured. Every other feature of the singer's education is simply a matter of time and application. But, under present conditions, the acquirement of the correct vocal action is extremely uncertain. On account of its fundamental importance, and more especially of its difficulty, the subject of tone-production is the most prominent topic of instruction in singing. The term "method" is therefore applied solely to the means used for imparting the correct vocal action.

This use of the word is in accordance with the accepted theory of Voice Culture. The general belief is that tone-production is entirely distinct from vocal technique. Technical studies cannot profitably be undertaken, according to the prevailing idea, until the correct management of the vocal organs has been established. This idea is supposed to be followed out in modern instruction. It is generally assumed that the voice is brought under control through a definite series of exercises; these exercises are supposed to follow, one after the other, according to a well-defined system. The term "method" implies this systematic arrangement of exercises. It indicates that vocal training is a matter of precise knowledge and orderly progression.

This represents the accepted ideal of Voice Culture, rather than the actual condition. The idea that the vocal management should be imparted specially, as something preliminary to the technical training of the voice, is not carried out in practice. Teachers generally are striving to bring their systems into conformity with this ideal standard. They use the expression, "placing the voice," to describe the preliminary training in tone-production. But no successful system of this type has ever been evolved. The correct management of the voice never is imparted in the manner indicated by this ideal of instruction. Tone-production continues, throughout the entire course of study, to be the most important topic of instruction.

In order to understand the nature of a method of Voice Culture, it is necessary first to consider the relation which exists, in modern instruction, between training in tone-production, and the development of vocal technique. According to the accepted theory, the voice must be "placed" before the real study of singing is undertaken. After the voice has been properly "placed," it is supposed to be in condition to be developed by practice in singing technical exercises. But in actual practice this distinction between "voice-placing" exercises and technical studies is seldom drawn. The voice is trained, almost from the beginning of the course of study, by practice in actual singing. The earliest exercises used for "placing the voice" are in every respect technical studies,--single tones and syllables, scale passages, arpeggios, etc. It is impossible to produce even a single tone without embodying some feature of technique. Practice therefore serves a double purpose; it brings the voice gradually to the condition of perfect action, and at the same time it develops the technique. The student advances gradually toward the correct manner of tone-production, and this progress is evidenced solely by the improved technical use of the voice. Considerable technical facility is attained before the tone-production becomes absolutely perfect.

A vocal student's practice in singing is not confined to technical exercises, strictly speaking. Vocalises, songs, and arias are taken up, usually very early in the course of study. Moreover, attention is nearly always paid to musical expression and to artistic rendition, as well as to the vocal action and the technical use of the voice. This is true, whether the student sings an exercise, a vocalise, a song, or an aria.

For daily home practice, the student sings, usually, first some exercises, then a few vocalises, and finally several songs and arias. Every teacher has at command a wide range of compositions of all these kinds, carefully graded as to technical and musical difficulty. As the pupil advances, more and more difficult works are undertaken. For each stage of advancement the teacher chooses the compositions best adapted to carry the student's progress still further.

There is no point in this development at which instruction in tone-production ceases, and the technical training of the voice is begun. On the contrary, the means used for imparting the correct vocal action are interspersed with the other materials of instruction, both technical and artistic, throughout the entire course of study. Moreover, the training in tone-production is carried on during the singing of the compositions just described, as well as by practice on "voice-placing" exercises strictly speaking.

A method of instruction in singing therefore consists primarily of a set of mechanical rules and directions for managing the voice, and secondarily of a series of exercises, both toneless and vocal, so designed that the student may directly apply in practising them the rules and directions for vocal management. It must not be understood however that the mechanical rules are applied only to the exercises specially designed for this purpose. These rules and directions are also intended to be applied to everything the student sings,--exercises, technical studies, and musical compositions.

It will be recalled that the review of the topics of modern vocal instruction covered three distinct types of materials. First, the purely mechanical doctrines, commonly regarded as the only strictly scientific principles of Voice Culture. These are, the rules for the management of the breath, of the registers, of laryngeal action, and of the resonance cavities, and also the directions for attacking the tone, and for forward emission. The second class of materials is held by strict adherents of the scientific idea to be purely empirical; this class includes the traditional precepts of the old Italian school, and also all the topics of instruction based on the singer's sensations. A third class of materials is found in the attempts to interpret the empirical doctrines in the light of the scientific analysis of the vocal action.

To enumerate and classify all the methods of instruction in vogue would be almost an impossibility. Absolutely no uniformity can be found on any topic. Even among the accepted doctrines of Vocal Science there are many controverted points. Five distinct schools of breathing are represented, two of breath-control. Of well worked-out systems of registers, at least twenty could be enumerated. Fully this number of theories are offered regarding the correct positions of the larynx, soft palate, and tongue. Two opposed theories are held as to nasal resonance. Further, the empirical doctrines are always stated so loosely that no real unanimity of view can be found on any one of them.

Every vocal teacher selects the materials of instruction from these controverted doctrines, but neither rule nor reason determines what materials shall be embodied in any one method. There is no coherence whatever in the matter. Further, there is no agreement as to which topics of instruction are most important. One teacher may emphasize breath-control and support of tone as the foundations of the correct vocal action, another may give this position to nasal resonance and forward placing. Yet both these teachers may include in their methods about the same topics. The methods seem entirely different, only because each makes some one or two doctrines the most important. In short, it might almost be said that there are as many methods as teachers.

Three fairly distinct types of method may be defined, depending on the class of materials adopted. At one extreme are found those teachers who attempt to follow strictly the scientific principles. These teachers generally profess to employ only the purely mechanical doctrines of Vocal Science, and to ignore all empirical interpretations of these doctrines. They generally devote a portion of every lesson to toneless muscular drills, and insist that their pupils practise every exercise in singing, with special attention to the throat action. These teachers attempt to follow a definite plan and order in the giving of exercises and rules. This systematic arrangement of instruction is, however, seldom followed out consistently with any one student. An important reason for this is considered in Chapter I of

Part II.

A very different type of method is taught by many teachers who pay special attention to the empirical topics of instruction. Of course no teacher professes to teach empirically; on the contrary, every method is called scientific, no matter what materials it embodies. Indeed, a very little attention paid to breathing, attack, registers, and nasal resonance, is enough to relieve any teacher of the reproach of empiricism. The teachers now being considered touch to some extent on these topics; but most of their instruction is based on the traditional precepts, the singer's sensations, and the special vowel and consonant drills. In the first few lessons of the course they usually give some special breathing exercises, but almost always ignore breath-control. Not much is done for vocal control in the strictly muscular sense. Special "voice-placing" exercises are not used to any such extent as in the strictly scientific methods just described, the voice-placing work being usually done on vocalises, songs, and arias. No system whatever is followed, or even attempted, in the sequence of topics touched upon. The directions, "Breathe deeper on that phrase," "Bring that tone more forward," "Open your throat for that ah," "Feel that tone higher up in the head," may follow one after the other within five minutes of instruction.

Teachers of this type are frequently charged, by the strict advocates of mechanical instruction, with a practice commonly known as "wearing the voice into place." This expression is used to indicate the total abandonment of system in imparting the correct vocal action. It means that the teacher simply has the pupil sing at random, trusting to chance, or to some vague intuitive process, to bring about the correct use of the voice. To the vocal scientist, "wearing the voice into place" represents the depth of empiricism.

The great majority of teachers occupy a middle ground between the two types just described. Teachers of this class touch, more or less, on every topic of instruction, mechanical, empirical, and interpretive. Their application of most of the topics of instruction is not quite so mechanical as in the first type of method considered. The student's attention is always directed to the vocal organs, but the idea of direct muscular control is not so consistently put forward. As a rule, the attempt is made in the first stages of instruction to follow a systematic plan. Breathing, and perhaps breath-control, are first taught as muscular drills, and then applied on single tones. Attack is generally taken up next, then simple exercises in the medium register. Following this, the chest and head registers are placed, and the attention is turned to emission and resonance. But in most cases, when the pupil has covered three or four terms of twenty lessons each, all system is abandoned. The method from that time on is about of the type described as empirical.

It must be remembered that this classification of methods is at best very crude. It would not be easy to pick out any one teacher who adheres consistently to any of the three forms of instruction described. All that can be said is that a teacher usually tends somewhat more to one type than to another.

Further, the degree of prominence given to the idea of direct mechanical control of the voice does not classify a method quite satisfactorily. Without exception every teacher adheres to the prevailing idea, that the voice must be controlled and guided in some direct way,--that the singer "must do something" to cause the vocal organs to operate properly. All the materials of instruction, mechanical and empirical, are utilized for the sole purpose of enabling the student to learn how to "do this something."

Several names are used by teachers to describe their methods. One professes to teach a "natural method," another the "pure Italian school of Bel Canto," a third the "old Italian method as illustrated by Vocal Science," a fourth the "strict scientific system of Voice Culture." No attention need be paid to these expressions, as they are seldom accurate descriptions.

Vocal lessons are usually of thirty minutes' duration. Each student generally takes two such lessons every week, although in some cases three, four, or even more are taken. A description of a few typical lessons will show how the materials of instruction are practically utilized.

Example 1: The student takes a few preliminary toneless breaths. Then follow, in the order given, a few short tones for practice on attack, some sustained tones on the vowel ah, exercises on three, four, and five notes, ascending and descending, a single tone followed by the octave jump up and descending scale, this last rising by semitones through several keys. In these exercises the student's attention is directed at random to the correct use of the registers, to nasal resonance, forward emission, etc. This consumes ten or twelve minutes of the lesson time. More elaborate exercises on scale passages are then sung, lasting another five minutes. These are followed by a vocalise or two, and a couple of songs or arias, which fill out the thirty minutes.

Example 2: A few breathing exercises are practised, followed by single tones and short scale passages, the whole lasting about five minutes. Then the student is drilled for some ten minutes on "placing the head tones," in the manner described in the section on special vowel and consonant drills. These exercises are varied by swelling the high tone, by changing the vowels, and by elaborating the descending scale passages. The remaining fifteen minutes are devoted to vocalises and songs.

Example 3: This is an advanced pupil, whose voice is supposed to be fairly well "placed." Technical exercises of some difficulty are sung, covering a range of an octave and a half, or a little more. The teacher interrupts occasionally to say "Sing those lower notes more in the chest voice," "Place the upper notes higher in the head," "Don't let your vocal cords open on that ah," "Sing that again and make the tones cleaner," etc. One or two arias are then sung, interspersed with instructions of the same sort, and also with suggestions regarding style, delivery, and expression.

For daily practice between lessons, the student sings usually the same exercises and studies included in the previous lesson, and also commits to memory compositions assigned for future study.

Examples of this kind might be multiplied indefinitely, but the main points have been fairly well brought out. Most important to be noticed is the fact that the voice is trained by practice in actual singing. In the whole scheme of modern Voice Culture, toneless muscular drills consume only an insignificant proportion of the time devoted to lessons. Further, the number of exercises and musical compositions embraced in a single half-hour lesson is very small. On the other hand, no limit can be set to the number of topics of vocal control touched on in any one lesson. These latter are used, throughout the whole range of instruction, without any systematic sequence. Whatever fault of production the pupil's tones indicate, the teacher calls attention to the fault, and gives the supposedly appropriate rule for its correction.

Part II

A CRITICAL ANALYSIS OF MODERN METHODS

CHAPTER I

MECHANICAL VOCAL MANAGEMENT AS THE BASIS OF VOICE CULTURE

Notwithstanding the wide diversity of opinion on most topics connected with vocal training, there is one point on which all authorities agree. This is, that the voice must be consciously controlled. In all the conflict of methods, this basic mechanical idea has never been attacked. On the contrary, it is everywhere accepted without question as the foundation of all instruction in singing.

The idea of mechanical vocal control is also the starting-point of all analysis of the vocal action. Every investigator of the voice approaches the subject in the belief that an exact determination of the muscular operations of correct singing would lead to an absolutely infallible method of training voices. The problem of tone-production is identical, in the common belief, with the problem of the vocal action. Three sciences, anatomy, mechanics, and acoustics, are believed to hold somewhere among them the secret of the voice. All investigation has therefore been carried on along the lines of these three sciences. It is on this account that modern methods are called scientific, and not because they are in conformity with general scientific principles. Before taking up the question whether the idea of mechanical vocal control is well grounded in fact and reason, let us consider further the influence of this idea on modern methods of instruction.

All instruction in singing is intended to teach the student to "do something," in order that the vocal organs may be directly caused to act properly. No matter how vague and indefinite the directions given, their aim is always to inform the student what to do, how to guide the vocal action. Even when used in a purely empirical way the directions for open throat, etc., are always given in this spirit. That these directions are utterly meaningless in the mechanical sense does not alter the fact; nobody has ever found any other connection in which they would take on a definite meaning.

In this regard the empirical directions are no more unsatisfactory than the mechanical doctrines of the accepted Vocal Science. It was pointed out that no means has ever been discovered for applying several of these doctrines in practical instruction. The rules contained in the theoretical works on Voice Culture for managing the registers and vocal-cord action, for forward emission of tone, and for control of the resonance cavities, are of no value whatever to the student of singing. It will be asked, how does the conscientious teacher get over this difficulty? How are the deficiencies of the scientific doctrines supplied in instruction? In many cases the deficiency is absolutely ignored. The student is simply told to "make the vocal cords act properly," to "direct the tone against the roof of the mouth," to "bring in the nasal resonance," etc., and no further help is given. That this works severe hardship on the earnest student need hardly be mentioned.

Other teachers, as has been explained, rely on a description of the singer's sensations, and on the use of several vowel and consonant combinations, for imparting control of resonance and forward emission. These means are purely empirical makeshifts, and as a rule they are not sanctioned by the consistent advocates of scientific instruction. But for acquiring control of the correct vocal-cord action, absolutely no means has ever been found, scientific or empirical. On this, the surpassingly important feature of the vocal action, Vocal Science has thrown no light whatever.

It was also remarked that the strictly scientific idea of Voice Culture is very seldom carried out, to its logical conclusion, in actual instruction. One important reason for this is that a student seldom remains long enough with a teacher to cover the entire ground of mechanical instruction. Students move about from teacher to teacher. In the class of any one master the proportion of pupils who have never had any previous instruction does not average one in ten. To carry the idea of averages further, the length of time a student takes lessons of one instructor may be set down as seldom more than two years.

How long it would take to apply the complete system of mechanical vocal training has never been precisely stated. Cases are on record of pupils being kept on mechanical drills and elementary exercises for four years, without being allowed to attempt a simple song. But these instances are extremely rare. It seldom happens that a teacher can hold a pupil long enough to carry out the complete course of mechanical study.

There are however many teachers who try conscientiously to have their pupils pay attention to all the mechanical features of the vocal action. What it would mean to sing in this way can only be imagined. Before starting a tone, the singer would prepare by taking a breath in some prescribed way, and retaining this breath an instant by holding the chest walls out. Meanwhile the lips, tongue, soft palate, and larynx would each be placed in the correct position. The jaw would be held relaxed, and the throat loose and open. The expected tone would be felt, in imagination, high up in the head, to assure the proper influence of nasal resonance. The vocal cords would be held in readiness to respond instantly to the mental command, so as to assure the exact state of tension necessary. Preparation would be made to direct the "column of vocalized breath," through the pharynx and mouth, to the proper point on the hard palate. Then, at the same precise instant, the breath would be started, and the vocal cords would be brought together, but without touching.

So the tone would be begun. And all this would have to be done, with due attention to each operation, in the fraction of a second preceding the starting of the tone! The downright absurdity of this idea of singing must be apparent to any one who has ever listened to a great singer.

Under the influence of the idea of mechanical vocal management there is little room for choice between voice culture along empirical lines, and the accepted type of scientific instruction. Modern empirical voice training has little practical value. Describing to the student the sensations which ought to be felt, does not help in the least. Even if the sensations felt by the singer, in producing tone correctly, are entirely different from those accompanying any incorrect use of the voice, nothing can be learned thereby. The sensations of correct singing cannot be felt until the voice is correctly used. An effect cannot produce its cause. Correct tone-production must be there to cause the sensations, or the sensations are not awakened at all. Nothing else can bring about the sensations of correct singing, but correct singing itself.

Further, these sensations cannot be known until they are actually experienced. No description is adequate to enable the student to feel them in imagination. And, finally, even if the sensations could be described with all vividness, imagining them would not influence the vocal organs in any way. This is true, whether the description is given empirically, or whether it is cited to explain a mechanical feature of the vocal action. Instruction based on the singer's sensations is absolutely valueless.

It would seem that modern methods contain very little of real worth. The investigation of the mechanical operations of the voice can hardly be said to have brought forth anything of definite value to the vocal teacher. But this is not the worst that can be said about the mechanical doctrines of tone-production. When critically examined, and submitted to a rigid scientific analysis, several of these doctrines are found to be erroneous in conception. These are the theories of breath-control, chest resonance, nasal resonance, and emission of tone. It will be observed that these doctrines comprise more than half of the materials of the accepted Vocal Science. Yet notwithstanding the fact that they are accepted without question by the great majority of vocal theorists as important elements of instruction in singing, each of these doctrines involves a distinct misconception of scientific principles. An examination of these doctrines is therefore the next subject to be undertaken.

CHAPTER II

THE FALLACY OF THE DOCTRINE OF BREATH-CONTROL

When Dr. Mandl advanced the statement that the laryngeal muscles are too weak to withstand the pressure of a powerful expiratory blast, the theory of the vocal action therein embodied met with immediate acceptance. This idea is so plausible that it appeals to the thoughtful investigator as self-evident, and seems to call for no proof. The doctrine of breath-control was at once adopted, by the most influential vocal scientists, as the basic principle of tone-production.

Curiously, neither Dr. Mandl, nor any other advocate of breath-control, seems to have read an article by Sir Charles Bell dealing with this same action, the closing of the glottis against a powerful exhalation. This paper, "On the Organs of the Human Voice," was read before a meeting of the London Philosophical Society on February 2, 1832.

Dr. Bell dispels all the mystery concerning the closure of the glottis, and the holding of the breath against a powerful contraction of the expiratory muscles. He points out that this action occurs in accordance with the law of the distribution of pressure in a fluid body, commonly known as Pascal's law of fluid pressures.

Pascal's law is stated as follows:--"Pressure exerted anywhere upon a mass of fluid is transmitted undiminished in all directions, and acts with equal force on all equal surfaces, and in a direction at right angles to those surfaces." (Atkinson's Ganot's Physics, 4th ed., New York, 1869.)

The hydraulic press furnishes the familiar illustration of this law. Two vertical cylinders, one many times larger than the other, are connected by a pipe. The cylinders are fitted with pistons. Both the cylinders, and the pipe connecting them, are filled with water, oil, air, or any other fluid; the fluid can pass freely from one cylinder to the other, through the connecting pipe. Suppose a horizontal section of the smaller cylinder to measure one square inch, that of the larger to be one hundred square inches. A weight of one pound on the smaller piston will balance a weight of one hundred pounds on the larger. If a downward pressure of one pound be exerted on the smaller piston, the larger piston will exert an upward pressure of one hundred pounds. Conversely, a downward pressure of one hundred pounds, exerted on the larger piston, will effect an upward pressure of only one pound on the smaller piston.

A type of the hydraulic press is presented by the chest cavity and the larynx, considered as one apparatus. This fact is illustrated in the following quotation: "If a bladder full of water be connected with a narrow upright glass tube, heavy weights placed on the bladder will be able to uphold only a very small quantity of liquid in the tube, this arrangement being in fact a hydraulic press worked backwards. If the tube be shortened down so as to form simply the neck of the bladder, the total expulsive pressure exerted by the bladder upon the contents of the neck may seem to be very small when compared with the total pressure exerted over the walls of the bladder upon the whole contents." (A Text Book of the Principles of Physics, Alfred Daniell, London, 1884.)

That the glottis-closing muscles are too weak to withstand a powerful expiratory pressure is therefore an entirely erroneous statement. Owing to the small area of the under surfaces of the vocal cords, the air pressure against them is very small, in comparison with the total pressure exerted on the contents of the thorax by the expiratory contraction. The glottis-closing muscles are fully capable of withstanding this comparatively slight pressure. The doctrine of breath-control is therefore scientifically untenable. This doctrine has no place in Vocal Science.

As the basic doctrine of breath-control is unsound, the singer does not need any direct means for controlling the breath. The attempt to check the flow of the breath in any mechanical way is entirely uncalled for. This being the case, it is hardly to be expected that the systems devised to meet this fancied need would stand the test of scientific examination. Each of these systems of breath-control, opposed muscular action and ventricular, is in fact found on analysis to embody a misconception of scientific principles.

Opposed-Action Breath-Control

A curious misapprehension of mechanical processes is contained in the doctrine of breath-control by opposed muscular action. This can best be pointed out by a consideration of the forces brought to bear on a single rib in the acts of inspiration and expiration. One set of muscles contract to raise this rib in inspiration, an opposed set, by their contraction, lower the rib for the act of expiration. In the opposed-action system of breath-control, the action of the rib-raising muscles is continued throughout the expiration, as a check upon the pull in the opposite direction of the rib-lowering muscles. Theoretically, the downward pull is "controlled" by the upward pull. To express this idea in figures, let the expiratory or downward pull on the rib be said to involve the expenditure of five units of strength. According to the theory of opposed-action breath-control, this downward pull would have to be opposed by a slightly less upward pull, say four units of strength.

Thus graphically presented, the fallacy of the "opposed-muscular" theory is clearly exposed. The rib is lowered with a degree of strength equal to the excess of the downward over the upward pull. If the downward pull equals five units of strength, and the upward pull four units, the rib is lowered with a pull equivalent to one unit of strength. Exactly the same effect would be obtained if the downward and upward pulls were equal respectively to twenty and nineteen units, or to two and one units. Further, the result would be the same if the downward pull involved the exertion of one unit of strength, and there was no upward pull whatever. In every case, the actual result is equivalent to the excess of the downward over the upward pull.

In the case of the expiratory pressure of five units of strength being "controlled" by an inspiratory contraction of four units, nine units of strength are exerted, and the same result could be obtained by the exertion of one unit. There is a clear waste of eight units of strength. The power of the expiratory blast is just what it would be if one unit of strength were exerted in an "uncontrolled" expiration. The singer exerts just nine times as much strength as is necessary to effect the same result. This is why the practice of breath-control exercises is so extremely fatiguing.

So far as the effect of the expiratory blast on the vocal cords is concerned, "controlling" the breath has no influence whatever. The vocal cords respond to the effective air pressure; they are not affected in any way by the opposed contractions of the breath muscles. "Opposed-muscular" breath-control is a sheer waste of time and effort.

Probably no particular harm has ever resulted to any singer's throat from the practice of breath-control exercises. But the attempt to hold back the breath has a very bad effect on the singer's delivery. The "breath-control" type of singer is never found in the ranks of the great artists. There is something utterly unnatural about this holding back of the breath, repugnant to every singer endowed with the right idea of forceful and dramatic delivery. The vast majority of the successful pupils of "breath-control" teachers abandon, very early in their careers, the tiresome attempt to hold back the breath. These singers yield, probably unconsciously, to the instinctive impulse to sing freely and without constraint.

But in the ranks of the minor concert and church singers are many who try conscientiously to obey the instructions of the "breath-control" teachers. Singers of this type can always be recognized by a curious impression of hesitancy, or even timidity, conveyed by their tones. They seem afraid to deliver their phrases with vigor and energy; they do not "let their voices out." Frequently their voices are of excellent quality, and their singing is polished and refined. But these singers never give to the listener that sense of satisfaction which is felt on hearing a fine voice freely and generously delivered.

As for the particular fallacy contained in the theory of ventricular breath-control, that must be reserved for a later chapter. Suffice it to say here that this theory disregards the two basic mechanical principles of tone-production,--Pascal's law, and the law of the conservation of energy. The application of this latter physical law to the operations of the vocal organs is considered in Chapter VI of Part III.

CHAPTER III

THE FALLACIES OF FORWARD EMISSION, CHEST RESONANCE, AND NASAL RESONANCE

Sir Morell Mackenzie's analysis of the acoustic principle supposedly involved in "forward emission" has already been quoted. That this analysis involves a complete misunderstanding of the laws of acoustics need hardly be said. When stated in precise terms, the fallacy of the "forward emission" theory is evident:

"On issuing from the vocal cords the tone is directed in a curved path, around the back of the tongue. There the tone is straightened out, and made to impinge on the roof of the mouth at a precisely defined point. From this point the tone is reflected, not directly back, as it should be, since the angles of incidence and reflection must be equal. Instead of this, the tone is reflected forward, out of the mouth, necessarily again taking a curved path, to avoid striking the front teeth." Naturally, no muscular action has ever been defined for causing the tone to perform this remarkable feat.

The "forward emission" theory assumes the existence of a current of air, issuing from the vocal cords as a tone. In other words, the tone is supposed to consist of a stream of air, which can be voluntarily directed in the mouth, and aimed at some precise point on the roof of the mouth. This is an utter mistake.

There is no "column of vibrating air," or "stream of vocalized breath," in the mouth during tone-production. In the acoustic sense, the air in the mouth-pharynx is still air, not air in a current. The only motion which takes place in the air in this cavity is the oscillatory swing of the air particles. To imagine the directing of air vibrations in the mouth, as we direct a stream of water out of a hose, is absurd.

What then is the "forward tone"? There must be some reason for this well-known effect of a perfectly produced voice,--the impression made on the hearer that the tones are formed in the front of the mouth. There ought also to be some way for the singer to learn to produce tones of this character. A consideration of this feature of the vocal action is reserved for Chapter IV of part III.

Chest Resonance

Who was originally responsible for the doctrine of chest resonance, it would be impossible now to determine. Were it not for the fact of this doctrine having received the support of eminent scientists (Holmes, Mackenzie, Curtis, and many others), it might be looked upon as a mere figure of speech. That the tones of the voice are reinforced by the resonance of the air in the chest cavity, is an utter absurdity. In the acoustic sense, the thorax is not a cavity at all. The thorax is filled with the spongy tissue of the lungs, not to mention the heart. It is no better adapted for air resonance than an ordinary spherical resonator would be, if filled with wet sponges.

Nasal Resonance

Enough was said of the theories of nasal resonance in Chapter IV of

Part I to show the unscientific character of all these theories. It remains only to point out the misconception of acoustic principles, contained in all the discussions of the subject. This is very much the same as in the theory of "forward emission," viz., that the tones of the voice consist physically of a "stream of vocalized breath." The mistaken idea is, that nasal resonance results from part or all of the expired breath passing through the nose.

What is nasal resonance? How is it caused? What is its effect on the tones of the voice? These questions have never been answered. It can however be proved that a satisfactory science of Voice Culture is not in any way dependent on obtaining an answer to these questions. This much is definitely known:

1. If the resonance of the air in the nasal cavities exerts any influence on the tones of the voice, this influence cannot be increased, diminished, or prevented by any direct action on the part of the singer. Shutting off the entrance of the breath, by raising the soft palate, is possible as a muscular exercise. But it is impossible to perform this action, and to sing artistically, at the same time. To produce any kind of tone, while holding the soft palate raised, is extremely difficult. In a later chapter it will be seen that this action has no place whatever in the correct use of the voice.

2. As the nasal cavities are fixed in size and shape, the singer cannot control or vary any influence which they may exert as a resonator.

3. Independent of any thought or knowledge of how the nasal quality of tone is caused, the singer has perfect voluntary control over this quality by the simple, direct influence of the will. A singer may produce nasal tones, or tones free from this faulty sound, at will, with no thought of the mechanical processes involved. All that is required is that the singer have an ear keen enough to recognize the nasal quality in his own voice, as well as in the voice of any other singer.

CHAPTER IV

THE FUTILITY OF THE MATERIALS OF MODERN METHODS

Of the strictly scientific or mechanical materials of modern methods, four have been seen to be utterly erroneous. The remaining topics of instruction, mechanical and empirical, may with equal justice be submitted to a similar examination.

Several of these topics have already been critically examined. The rules for registers and laryngeal management were seen to be of no value to the student of singing. So also was it observed that all instruction which attempts to utilize the singer's sensations is futile. All that is left of the materials of modern methods, in which any valuable idea might be contained, are the rules for breathing.

Without undertaking to decide whether one system of breathing can be right, to the exclusion of all other systems, one general remark can be applied to the whole subject. It has never been scientifically proved that the correct use of the voice depends in any way on the mastery of an acquired system of breathing. True, this is the basic assumption of all the discussions of the singer's breathing. As Frangen-Davies justly remarks,--"All combatants are agreed on one point, viz., that the singer's breath is an acquired one of some kind." (The Singing of the Future, David Frangen-Davies, M.A., London, 1906.) This is purely an assumption on the part of the vocal theorists. No one has ever so much as attempted to offer scientific proof of the statement.

Further, it is frequently stated that the old Italian masters paid much attention to the subject of breathing; the assumption is also made that these masters approached the subject in the modern spirit. Neither this statement, nor the assumption based on it, is susceptible of proof. Tosi and Mancini do not even mention the subject of breathing.

Breathing has been made the subject of exhaustive mechanical and muscular analysis, for one reason, and for only one reason. This is, because the action of breathing is the only mechanical feature of singing which can be exhaustively studied. The laryngeal action is hidden; the influence of the resonance cavities cannot well be determined. But the whole muscular operation of breathing can be readily seen and studied; any investigator can personally experiment with every conceivable system.

Furthermore, the adoption of any system of breathing has no influence whatever on the operations of the voice. A student of singing may learn to take breath in any way favored by the instructor; the manner of tone-production is not in the least affected. Even if the correct use of the voice has to be acquired, the mode of breathing does not contribute in any way to this result.

All that need be said in criticism of the various doctrines of breathing is, that the importance of this subject has been greatly overestimated. Breath and life are practically synonymous. Nothing but the prevalence of the mechanical idea has caused so much attention to be paid to the singer's breathing. A tuba player will march for several hours in a street parade, carrying his heavy instrument, and playing it fully half the time; yet the vocal theorist does not consider him an object of sympathy.

No doubt the acquirement of healthy habits of breathing is of great benefit to the general health. But this does not prove that correct singing demands some kind of breathing inherently different from ordinary life. To inspire quickly and exhale the breath slowly is not an acquired ability; it is the action of ordinary speech. Singing demands that the lungs be filled more quickly than in ordinary speech, and perhaps a fuller inspiration is also required. This is readily mastered with very little practice. It does not call for the acquirement of any new muscular movements, nor the formation of any new habits.

What is left of all the materials of modern vocal instruction? To sum them up in the order in which they were considered in

Part I:

Breathing does not need to be mastered in any such way as is stated in the theoretical works on the voice. Breath-control is a complete fallacy. The doctrines of registers and laryngeal action are utterly valueless. Chest resonance, nasal resonance, and forward emission, are scientifically erroneous. The traditional precepts are of no value, because nobody knows how to follow or apply them. Empirical teaching based on the singer's sensations is of no avail.

In other words, modern methods contain not one single topic of any value whatever in the training of the voice. It will be objected that this statement is utterly absurd, because many of the world's greatest singers have been trained according to these methods. No doubt this is in one sense true; modern methods can point to many brilliant successes. But this does not prove anything in favor of the materials of modern methods.

Singers are trained to-day exactly as they were trained two hundred years ago, through a reliance on the imitative faculty. The only difference is this: In the old days, the student was directly and expressly told to listen and to imitate, while to-day the reliance on the imitative faculty is purely instinctive. A fuller consideration of the important function of imitation as an unrecognized element of modern Voice Culture is contained in Chapter V of Part IV.

CHAPTER V

THE ERROR OF THE THEORY OF MECHANICAL VOCAL MANAGEMENT

A fundamental difference was pointed out, at the close of the preceding chapter, between the old Italian method and modern systems of vocal instruction. This is worthy of repetition. The old Italian method was founded on the faculty of imitation. Modern methods have as their basis the idea of conscious, direct, mechanical control of the vocal organs. All the materials of instruction based on this idea of mechanical control were seen to be absolutely valueless. It is now in order to examine still further the structure of modern Voice Culture, and to test this basic idea of mechanical control.

As a muscular operation, the actions of singing must be subject to the same physiological and psychological laws which govern all other voluntary muscular actions. What are these laws? How do we guide and control our muscular movements? At first sight, this seems a simple question. We know what we want to do, and we do it. But the important point is, how are we able to do the things we want to do? You wish to raise your hand, for example, therefore you raise it. How does your hand know that you wish to raise it? Does the hand raise itself? Not at all; it is raised by the contraction of certain muscles in the arm, shoulder, and back. That is, when you wish to raise your hand, certain muscles contract themselves. But these muscles are not part of the hand. What leads these muscles in the shoulder and back to contract, when you will to raise your hand? Normally you are not even aware of their contraction. Yet in some way these muscles know that they are called on to contract, in response to the wish to raise the hand. This takes place, even though you know nothing whatever of the muscles in question. The process is by no means so simple, when looked at in this light.

A complicated psychological process is involved in the simplest voluntary movements. This is seen in the following analysis:

"To move any part of the body voluntarily requires the following particulars: (1) The possession of an educated reflex-motor mechanism, under the control of the higher cerebral centers which are most immediately connected with the phenomena of consciousness; (2) certain motifs in the form of conscious feelings that have a tone of pleasure or pain, and so impel the mind to secure such bodily conditions as will continue or increase the one, and discontinue or diminish the other; (3) ideas of motions and positions of the bodily members, which previous experience has taught us answer more or less perfectly to the motifs of conscious feeling; (4) a conscious fiat of will, settling the question, as it were, which of these ideas shall be realized in the motions achieved and positions attained by these members; (5) a central nervous mechanism, which serves as the organ of relation between this act of will and the discharge of the requisite motor impulses along their nerve-tracts to the groups of muscles peripherally situated." (Elements of Physiological Psychology, Geo. T. Ladd, New York, 1889.)

Let us again consider the action of raising the hand, and see how the psychological analysis applies in this movement. We note in the first place that we are concerned only with the third, fourth, and fifth particulars of Prof. Ladd's analysis. These are:

The idea of the movement.

The fiat of will which directs that this movement be performed.

The discharge of the requisite motor impulses, along the nerve-tracts, to the muscles whose contraction constitutes the movement.

It will be simpler, and will answer the purpose equally well, to combine the third and fourth elements, and to consider as one element the idea of the movement and the fiat of will to execute the movement.

The Idea of a Movement

The mental picture of a purposed movement is simple and direct. No reference is involved to the muscles concerned in the performance of the movement. When you will to raise your hand, the action is pictured to your mind as the raising of the hand, and nothing more. Certain muscles are to be contracted. But the mental picture of the movement does not indicate what these muscles are, in what order they are to be brought into play, nor the relative degrees of strength to be exerted by each muscular fiber. You do not consciously direct the muscles in their contractions.

The Discharge to the Muscles of the Nerve Impulse

How then are the muscles informed that their contraction is called for? They have no independent volition; each muscular fiber obeys the impulse transmitted to it by the nerve, from the nerve center governing its action. These nerve centers are in their turn controlled by the central nervous mechanism. And in complex voluntary movements the central nervous mechanism is under the control of the higher cerebral centers. The wish to raise the hand appears to the mind as an idea of the hand being raised. This idea is translated by the central nervous mechanism into a set of motor nerve impulses. Does consciousness or volition come into play here? Not at all. On this point Prof. Ladd remarks: "As to the definite nature of the physical basis which underlies the connection of ideas of motion and the starting outward of the right motor impulses, our ignorance is almost complete."

Is it necessary for the performance of a complex muscular action that the individual know what muscles are involved and how and when to contract them? No; this knowledge is not only unnecessary, it is even impossible. Prof. Ladd says of this: "It would be a great mistake to regard the mind as having before it the cerebral machinery, all nicely laid out, together with the acquired art of selecting and touching the right nervous elements in order to produce the desired motion, as a skilful player of the piano handles his keyboard."

How then are the muscles informed of the service required of them? Or more precisely, how does the central nervous mechanism know what distribution of nerve impulses to make among the different nerve centers governing the muscles? As Prof. Ladd says, our ignorance on this point is almost complete. There resides in the central nervous mechanism governing the muscles something which for lack of a better name may be called an instinct. When a purposeful movement of any part of the body is willed, the mental picture of the movement is translated by the central nervous mechanism into a succession of nerve impulses; these impulses are transmitted through the lower centers to the muscles. The instinct informing the central nervous mechanism how to apportion the discharges of nerve impulse among the various muscular centers is to a high degree mysterious. The present purpose will not be served by carrying the analysis of this instinct further.[7]

[Note 7: The evolutionary development of this instinct is not altogether mysterious. Science can fairly well trace the successive steps in the development of the central nervous mechanism, from the amoeba to the highest type of vertebrate. "Nerve channels" are worn by the repeated transmission of impulses over the same tracts. Coordinations become in successive generations more complex and more perfect. As consciousness develops further, in each succeeding type, actions originally reflex tend to take on a more consciously purposeful character. But all we are concerned with now is the problem of tone-production. Our purpose is best served by accepting the faculty of muscular adaptation as an instinct, pure and simple.]

There is therefore no direct conscious guidance of the muscles, in any movement, simple or complex. So far as the command of voluntary muscular actions is concerned, the first simple statement of the process sums up all that for practical purposes need be determined;--we know what we want to do, and we do it. The mind forms the idea of an action and the muscles instinctively respond.

But the fact remains that the muscles need to be guided in some way. We do not perform instinctively many complex actions,--writing, dancing, rowing, swimming, etc. All these actions, and indeed most of the activities of daily life, must be consciously learned by practice and repeated effort. How are these efforts guided? To arrive at an answer to this question let us consider how a schoolboy practises his writing lesson.

The boy begins by having before him a copy of the letters he is to write. Under the guidance of the eye the hand traces these letters. At each instant the eye points out to the hand the direction in which to move. As the hand occasionally wanders from the prescribed direction the eye immediately notes the deviation and bids the hand to correct it. The hand responds to the demands of the eye, immediately, without thought on the boy's part of nerve impulse or of muscular contraction. By repeated efforts the boy improves upon his first clumsy attempts; with each repetition he approaches nearer to the model.

In the course of this progress the muscular sense gradually comes to the assistance of the eye as a sort of supplementary guidance. But at no time is the eye relieved of the responsibility of guiding the hand in writing. To sum this up, the movements of the hand in writing are guided, so far as the consciousness is aware, directly by the sense of sight.

We have here the law of voluntary muscular guidance. In all voluntary movements the muscles are guided in their contractions, through some instinctive process, by the sense or senses which observe the movements themselves, and more especially, the results of the movements. In most actions the two senses concerned are sight and muscular sense. The more an action becomes habitual the more it tends to be performed under the guidance of muscular sense, and to be free from the necessity of the guidance of the eye. But muscular sense does not usually rise so high into consciousness as sight, in the guidance of muscular activities. Many oft-repeated movements, especially those of walking, become thoroughly habitual and even automatic; that is, the muscular contractions are performed as purely reflex actions, without conscious guidance of any kind. But even in walking, the necessity may at any instant arise for conscious guidance. In such a case the sense of sight immediately comes into service; from reflex the movements become voluntary, and consciously guided. In the case of most complex actions the sense of sight furnishes the most important guidance.

If the muscular operations of singing are subject to the general laws of psychological control, the guidance of the vocal organs must be furnished by the sense which observes the results of the movements involved. This is the sense of hearing. Just as in writing the hand is guided by the eye, so in singing the voice is guided by the ear. There can be no other means of guiding the voice. Muscular sense may under certain conditions supplement the sense of hearing, but under no circumstances can muscular sense assume full command. The net result of the application of psychological principles to the problem of tone-production is simply this, that the voice is guided directly by the ear.

It is thus seen that the idea of mechanical vocal management is utterly erroneous. On pushing the analysis still further the fallacy of this idea is found to be even more glaring.

Is a knowledge of anatomy of any assistance in the acquirement of skill in performing complex muscular actions? Not in the least. An understanding of muscular processes does not contribute in any way to skilful execution. The anatomist does not play billiards or row a boat one whit the better for all his knowledge of the muscular structure of the body.

Even if the precise workings of the vocal mechanism could be determined, the science of Voice Culture would not benefit thereby. Knowing how the muscles should act does not help us to make them act properly. It is utterly idle to tell the vocal student that as the pitch of the voice rises the arytenoid cartilages rotate, bringing their forward surfaces together, and so shortening the effective length of the vocal cords. Whatever the vocal cords are required to do is performed through an instinctive obedience to the demands of the mental ear.

And finally, a precise analysis of muscular contractions is impossible, even in the case of comparatively simple actions. When, for example, the hand describes a circle in the air, a number of muscles are involved. True, it is known what these muscles are, and what effect the combined contractions of any group would have on the position of the hand. The direction of the hand's motion at any instant is determined by the resultant of all the forces exerted on this member. But as this direction constantly changes, so must the relative degrees of strength exerted by the muscles also constantly change. At no two successive instants are the muscular adjustments the same. This simple action, performed without thought or knowledge of the muscular processes, presents features too complex to be analyzed on the basis of mechanical law and anatomic structure.

A complete analysis of the muscular operations of tone-production is absolutely impossible. The adjustments of the laryngeal muscles involve probably the most minute variations in degree of contraction performed in the whole voluntary muscular system. What we do know of the mechanical operations of the voice is exceedingly interesting, and a further knowledge of the subject is greatly to be desired. But we can never hope to clear up all the mystery of the vocal action.

This statement must not be construed to mean that the study of the vocal mechanism has been devoid of valuable results. On the contrary, the present understanding of the mechanical operations of the voice will be found of very great value in erecting a true science of Voice Culture. The only weakness of the present results of vocal investigation is due to the fact that this investigation has always been carried on under the influence of the idea of mechanical vocal management. This influence has led all theoretical students of the subject to attempt to apply their knowledge in formulating rules for direct mechanical guidance of the voice. That these rules are valueless is due solely to the fundamental error involved in the mechanical idea.

Voice Culture must be turned from the idea of mechanical vocal management. The old Italian masters were right in that they relied, even though empirically, on the imitative faculty. Modern teachers may do better, for in the light of present knowledge reliance on the faculty of vocal imitation can be shown to be in strict accord with sound scientific principles.

Part III

THE BASIS OF A REAL SCIENCE OF VOICE

CHAPTER I

THE MEANS OF EMPIRICAL OBSERVATION OF THE VOICE

To all knowledge obtained through the observation of facts and phenomena, the term empirical is properly applied. Empirical knowledge must be the basis of every science. To be available in forming a science, empirical knowledge of a subject must be so carefully gathered that all probability of error is eliminated; the observations must be so exhaustive as to embrace every possible source of information. From the knowledge thus obtained a set of verified general rules must be worked out with which all the observed facts and phenomena are shown to be in accord. Then a science has been erected. There is no possibility of conflict between empirical and scientific knowledge. The discovery of a single fact, at variance with the supposed general laws bearing on any subject, is sufficient to overthrow the entire structure which had been accepted as a science.

In the accepted Vocal Science the terms empirical and scientific are used in a sense entirely different from that which properly attaches to these words. Present knowledge of the operations of the voice is called scientific, solely because it is derived from the sciences of anatomy, acoustics, and mechanics. The term "empirical knowledge of the voice" is used as a name for knowledge of the subject drawn from any source other than these sciences. Yet so far as the modern vocal world seems to be aware, it possesses no knowledge of the voice other than that commonly called scientific. It is supposed that the old Italian masters had some "empirical understanding of the voice." But, if this was the case, their empirical knowledge has apparently been utterly lost.

Thus far in the present work, the usage of the terms empirical and scientific, accepted by vocal theorists generally, has been adopted. A distinction has been drawn between knowledge of the voice obtained through the study of the vocal mechanism and that obtained through observation of any other kind. The purpose will best be served by continuing this same usage.

It must be apparent to the reader, from the analysis of modern methods, that no real Science of Voice has thus far been erected. This is due to the fact that the general principles of scientific investigation have not been applied to the study of the voice. Under the influence of the idea of mechanical vocal management the attention of all investigators has been turned exclusively to the mechanical features of tone-production. Meanwhile the empirical knowledge of the old masters seems to have been forgotten. As a matter of fact, as will now be seen, this empirical knowledge has never been lost. Every modern teacher of singing shares the empirical knowledge which formed the sole material of the old method. But this knowledge is not applied effectually in modern instruction for two reasons. First, modern teachers do not realize the importance of this knowledge; indeed, they are practically unaware of this valuable possession. Although in fact the basis of nearly all modern instruction in singing, empirical knowledge is always unconsciously used. Second, empirical knowledge is always applied in the prevailing mechanical spirit. The attempt is always made to translate the sub-conscious empirical understanding of the voice into rules for direct mechanical management. Under the influence of the mechanical idea the modern teacher's most valuable possession, empirical knowledge of the voice, becomes utterly unserviceable.

Thus far, the whole result of this work has been destructive. The accepted Vocal Science has been shown to be erroneous in its conception and unsound in its conclusions. The work cannot halt here. Vocal Science must be reconstructed. This can be done only by following the general plan of all scientific investigation, beginning with the observation of all ascertainable facts bearing on the voice.

How can any facts be observed about the voice other than by the study of the vocal mechanism? An answer to this question is at once suggested so soon as scientific principles are applied to the subject. Strictly speaking, the voice is a set of sounds, produced by the action of the vocal organs. The scientific method of inquiry is therefore to begin by observing these sounds. Sounds as such can be observed only by the sense of hearing. It follows then that the attentive listening to voices is the first step to be taken.

Can any empirical knowledge of the voice be obtained by the mere listening to voices? If so, we ought now to be in possession of any facts which might be thus observed. Is it possible that information of this character is already a common possession of the vocal world, and yet that this information has never been applied in the investigation of the voice? This is exactly the case. Many facts regarding the voice have been observed so continually that they are a matter of common knowledge, and yet these facts have never been recorded in a scientific manner.

Consider, for example, this remark about a famous singer, made by one of the foremost musical critics of the United States: "Mme. T---- 's lower medium notes were all sung with a pinched glottis." How did this critic know that the singer had pinched her glottis? He had no opportunity of examining her throat with the laryngoscope, nor of observing her throat action in any other way. In fact, the critic was seated probably seventy-five feet from the artist at the time the tones in question were sung. The critic had only one means of knowing anything about the singer's throat action, and that was contained in the sound of the tones. There must therefore have been something in the sound of the tones which conveyed this information to the critical listener. For many years this gentleman had been in the habit of listening closely to singers, and he had found some way of estimating the singer's throat action by the character of the tones produced.

This same means of judging the manner of production from the sound of the tones seems to have been utilized nearly two hundred years ago. Speaking of the most frequent faults of tone-production, Tosi remarks: "The voice of the scholar should always come forth neat and clear, without passing through the nose or being choked in the throat." Mancini also speaks of the faults of nasal and throaty voice: "Un cantare di gola e di naso." A throaty tone, therefore, impressed these writers as being in some way formed or caught in the singer's throat. It may be set down as certain that no pupil ever explained to either of these masters how the objectionable sounds were produced. How then did Tosi and Mancini know the manner in which a throaty tone is produced?

We need not go back to the early writers to find out what is meant by a throaty tone. Fully as many throaty singers are heard nowadays as the old masters ever listened to. What do we mean when we say that a singer's voice is throaty? The answer to this question seems at first sight simple enough: The tones impress us as being formed in the singer's throat. But what conveys this impression? Something in the sound of the tone, of course. Yet even that is not enough. How can a tone, merely a sound to which we listen, tell us anything about the condition of the singer's throat during the production of the tone? Here again the answer seems simple: The listener knows that, in order to produce a tone of like character, he would have to contract his own throat in some way.

Here we have a highly significant fact about the voice. On hearing a throaty tone, the listener can tell how this tone is produced; he feels that he would have to contract his own throat in order to produce a similar tone. Let us carry this discussion a little further. How does the listener know this? Certainly not by actually singing a throaty tone. When seated in a concert hall, for example, and listening to a throaty singer, the hearer cannot rise from his seat, sing a few throaty tones himself, and then note how his throat feels. The critic just mentioned did not sing some notes with "pinched glottis" in order to learn how Mme. T---- sang her low tones. Evidently it is not necessary actually to imitate the singer; the hearer gets the same result by imitating the sounds mentally. In other words, when we hear throaty tones we mentally imitate these tones; thus we know that we should have to contract our own throats in order to produce similar tones.

But even here we cannot stop. To imitate the singer actually is one thing; mental imitation is something entirely different. In the first case, actual imitation, our muscular sense would inform us of the state of throat tightening. But in the case of mental imitation there is no actual tightening of the throat, nothing, at any rate, comparable to what takes place in actual imitation. There is then a dual function of the imagination; first, the mental imitation of the sound; second, the imaginary tightening of the throat. The analysis of the mental process must therefore be modified, and stated as follows: When we listen to a throaty tone we mentally imitate the tone; an imaginative function of the muscular sense informs us what condition the singer's throat assumes for the production of the tone.

A similar operation takes place in listening to nasal voices. An impression is conveyed by a nasal tone, through which the hearer is informed of a condition of tightness or contraction somewhere in the singer's nose.

The terms applied to the two most marked forms of faulty tone-production, nasal and throaty, are derived from impressions conveyed by the sounds of the tones. These names, nasal and throaty, refer to a feeling of tightness or contraction experienced in imagination by the hearer; in one case this feeling is located in the nose, in the other, in the throat. But the terms nasal and throaty are general descriptions of faulty tones. Each one covers a wide range of tone qualities. There is an almost infinite variety of throaty tones, and of nasal sounds as well. The knowledge of the voice obtained by listening to vocal tones is of equally wide extent. Every throaty tone, whatever its precise character, informs the hearer of the exact condition of the singer's throat in producing the tone. In short, every vocal tone is thus analyzed by the critical listener, and referred in imagination to his own throat. An insight into the singer's vocal action is imparted to the hearer through an imaginative process which always, of necessity, accompanies the attentive listening to vocal tones.

Every vocal tone awakens in the hearer a set of imagined muscular sensations. These sensations furnish the means for an exhaustive analysis of the operations of the voice. The production of tone therefore awakens two sets of muscular sensations, one actually felt by the singer, the other felt in imagination by the listener. The former are commonly known as the "singer's sensations"; but, as will be explained later, this expression is often very loosely applied. It is advisable on this account to give a new name to the singer's sensations, and also to give a name to the muscular sensations awakened in the hearer. Let us therefore call the sensations experienced by the singer in the production of tone the "direct sensations of tone." To the imaginary sensations of the hearer let us give the name, the "sympathetic sensations of tone."

These two terms will be used throughout the remainder of this work in the meanings here given to them.

Direct sensations of tone are the sensations actually felt by the singer as a result of the exercise of the vocal organs.

Sympathetic sensations of tone are the muscular sensations experienced in imagination by the hearer as a result of the listening to the tones of voices other than his own.

CHAPTER II

SYMPATHETIC SENSATIONS OF VOCAL TONE

A peculiar relation of sympathy exists between the human voice and the human ear. So intimate is this relation that the two might almost be considered as forming one complete organ. One aspect of this relation has already been noted, the guidance of the vocal organs by the sense of hearing. There is now to be considered another feature of this relation between voice and ear,--the assistance rendered by the vocal organs to the sense of hearing.

That a sub-conscious adjustment of the vocal organs may supplement the sense of hearing in the estimation of pitch is mentioned by Prof. Ladd. Speaking of the ability, by no means uncommon, to tell the pitch of any musical note heard, Prof. Ladd says: "Such judgment, however, may be, and ordinarily is, much assisted by auxiliary discriminations of other sensations which blend with those of the musical tone. Among such secondary helps the most important are the muscular sensations which accompany the innervation of the larynx and other organs used in producing musical tones. For we ordinarily innervate these organs (at least in an inchoate and partial way)--that is, we sound the note to ourselves--when trying carefully to judge of its pitch." (Elements of Physiological Psychology.)

Much more important in the study of the problem of tone-production are the adjustments of the hearer's vocal organs which were named the sympathetic sensations of tone. This peculiar auxiliary to the sense of hearing calls for the closest attention.

Sympathetic sensations of tone are awakened in the hearer through the mere listening to the sounds of the human voice. Vocal tones impress the listener's ear in a manner entirely different from any other sounds. Not only are the tones of the voice heard, just as other sounds are heard; in addition to this, every vocal tone heard is mentally imitated, and this mental reproduction of the tone is referred in imagination to the hearer's own vocal organs. Besides hearing the vocal tone as a sound pure and simple, the listener is also informed of the manner of throat action by which the tone is produced.

This mental imitation and judgment of vocal tones is not a voluntary operation. On the contrary it cannot even be inhibited. It is impossible for us to listen to the voices of those about us, even in ordinary conversation, without being to some extent aware of the various modes of tone-production.

This idea of the mental imitation of voices may impress us at first as highly mysterious. Sympathetic sensations of tone have been felt and noted, probably ever since the human voice and the human ear were developed. Yet the process is purely sub-conscious. It is performed involuntarily, without thought on the part of the hearer, even without any consciousness of the process. The hearer simply knows how the voices to which he listens are produced. A throaty voice simply sounds throaty; the hearer feels this, and pays no attention to the source of the information. We take it as a matter of course that a nasal voice seems to come through the speaker's nose. Why a certain quality of sound gives this impression we never stop to inquire. The impressions of throat action conveyed by other people's voices seem so simple and direct that nobody appears to have thought to analyze the psychological process involved.

This psychological process is found on analysis to be highly complex. In addition to the actual physical exercise of the sense of hearing, three distinct operations are performed in imagination. These are the mental imitation of the tone, the imagined adjustments of the vocal organs, and the imaginative exercise of the muscular sense. Although simultaneously performed, each of these four operations may be considered separately.

Hearing

As the judgment of vocal tones by sympathetic sensations is purely a function of the sense of hearing, the keenness of these sensations varies in each individual in proportion to the keenness of the ear. It would be a great mistake to assert that we all feel these sympathetic sensations with equal vividness. On the contrary, many people are so inattentive to the qualities of sounds that they hardly know the meaning of the term "nasal tone."

One trait in particular distinguishes the musician and the music lover; this is, the possession of a keen sense of hearing. The ear is trained by exercise in its own function,--hearing. The more attentively we listen to music the higher do we develop our ability to discriminate between musical sounds. Moreover, natural endowments vary in different individuals, with regard to the ear, as with all other human faculties. To appreciate fully the wonderful insight into vocal operations conveyed by the sympathetic sensations of tone, a naturally keen musical ear is required; further, this natural gift of a good ear must be developed by attentive listening to music, vocal and instrumental, carried on through several years.

Mental Imitation of Vocal Tones

That every sense has its counterpart in the imagination need hardly be said. We know what it means to feel warm or cold, hungry or thirsty; we know the taste of an apple, the scent of a rose. We can at will create pictures before the mind's eye. In the same way we can hear in imagination any sound we choose to produce mentally.

An inseparable function of the sense of hearing is the impulse to imitate mentally the tones of speakers and singers. The imitation of sounds is an instinctive operation. "Talking proper does not set in till the instinct to imitate sounds ripens in the nervous system." (The Principles of Psychology, Wm. James, N. Y., 1890.) Little can be said about the impulse to imitate voices mentally, further than that it is an exercise of this same instinct.

Imagined Adjustments of the Vocal Organs

It has already been seen that the vocal organs have the ability to adjust themselves, through instinctive guidance, for the production of any tone demanded by the ear. This same ability is invoked in the mental imitation of tones. In one case the muscular contractions are actually performed; in the other the muscular adjustments are wholly or in part imaginary.

It is highly probable that actual contractions of the laryngeal muscles take place, under certain conditions, as an accompaniment to the listening to voices. This is evident in the case of extremely aggravated throaty and forced voices. In listening to the harsh, raucous cries of many street vendors, when calling out their wares, the hearer frequently feels a sense of actual pain in his own throat.

Involuntary and unconscious contractions of the laryngeal muscles, somewhat similar to those under consideration, are well known to experimental psychologists. Prof. Ladd's statement that these contractions assist the ear in the judgment of absolute pitch has already been cited. Another example of unconscious laryngeal movements has been investigated by Hansen and Lehmann ("Ueber unwillkuerliches Fluestern," Philos. Studien,

1895, Vol. XI, p. 47), and by H. S. Curtis ("Automatic Movements of the Larynx," Amer. Jour. Psych., 1900, Vol. XI, p. 237). The laboratory experiments of these investigators show that when words, or ideas definitely expressed in words, are strongly thought but not uttered, the vocal organs unconsciously adjust themselves to the positions necessary for uttering the words. Curtis says of these unconscious laryngeal contractions: "Such movements are very common with normal people, and are comparatively easy of demonstration."

The apparatus used by Hansen and Lehmann in their experiments consists of two large concave reflectors. These are placed at a convenient distance, one facing the other, so that two experimenters may be seated, the first having his mouth at the focal point of one reflector, the second with his ear at the focal point of the other. As the first experimenter repeats mentally any words or phrases, these are found to be unconsciously whispered. These sounds of whispering, inaudible under ordinary conditions, are so magnified by the two reflectors as to be distinctly heard by the second experimenter.

Curtis proved that actual movements of the larynx unconsciously accompany intense thought. His demonstrations were conducted along lines familiar to all students of experimental psychology. Similar experiments would probably show that unconscious movements of the larynx also occur during the listening to vocal tones.

A peculiarity of the laryngeal adjustments accompanying the listening to voices is seen in the fact that the possession of a fine or well-trained voice is not required in this process. It does not matter whether the physical organs are capable of producing fine musical tones. The nervous equipment alone is involved; this is frequently highly developed, even though the physical voice is very poor. A keen and highly-trained ear is the only requisite. Players in the opera orchestras often develop this faculty to a high degree, even though they may never attempt to sing a note.

Muscular Sense

An exhaustive analysis of the various classes of sensations, commonly grouped under the general heading of muscular sense, would involve a mass of technicalities not necessary to the present purpose. It is sufficient to bear in mind the limitations of this sense, and to notice what it tells us, and what it does not tell.

Through the exercise of the muscular sense we are informed of the movements, positions, and conditions of the different parts of the body. Of specific muscular contractions very little information is conveyed. Thus, when the arm is bent at the elbow the muscular sensations of the movement are clear and definite; but, under normal conditions, these sensations do not inform us that the movement results from the contraction of the biceps muscle. Knowledge of the muscular structure of the body is not involved in muscular sense. The muscular sensations of bending the arm are felt in precisely the same way by the professor of anatomy and the ignorant child.

Further, no amount of attention paid to muscular sensations will inform us exactly what muscles are contracted in any complex action. A single stroke in the game of tennis, returning a swift service for example, may involve some contraction of every muscle of the entire body. A skilful player may observe with the utmost care the muscular sensations accompanying this stroke; he would never be able to learn from these sensations whether the number of muscles in his forearm is ten or one hundred.

For the same reason the sympathetic sensations of tone tell us nothing whatever of the muscular structure of the vocal organs. When listening to a throaty voice, we feel that the singer's throat is tightened, stiffened, or contracted. But no matter how keen and vivid this sensation may be, it leaves us in complete ignorance of the names and locations of the muscles wrongly contracted. This is true, however thoroughly we may know the anatomy of the vocal organs.

Much of the prevailing confusion about the voice is due to a misunderstanding of this point. When, for example, the musical critic asserted that Mme. T---- sang certain tones with "pinched glottis," he fell into this error. His sympathetic sensations informed him of some unnecessary tightening of the singer's throat. From these sensations he seems to have inferred that the glottis-closing muscles were too strongly contracted. This assumption was not warranted by any information conveyed in the sympathetic sensations.

It is not necessary now to determine to what extent the muscular sensations accompanying the listening to voices are purely imaginative, and to what extent they result from actual, though unconscious, contractions of the listener's throat muscles. The psychological process is the same in either case.

Sympathetic sensations of tone always accompany the listening to voices. While the psychological process is complex, this process is performed unconsciously and involuntarily. Even though the attention may be definitely turned to the sympathetic sensations themselves, the mental imitation and the laryngeal adjustments seldom rise into consciousness. As a rule, the entire operation is purely sub-conscious. The listener simply knows how the voices to which he listens are produced. This knowledge has always been accepted as intuitive; but this is merely another way of saying that the process of its acquirement is sub-conscious.

Direct Sensations of Tone

In addition to the source of misunderstanding of the vocal action just mentioned,--the attempt to define the precise muscular contractions indicated in the sympathetic sensations, another common misinterpretation of these sensations must be noted. As a consequence of the sub-conscious character of the sympathetic sensations, the two classes of muscular sensation of vocal tone, direct and sympathetic, are frequently confounded and classed together as the "singer's sensations." A third source of confusion is seen in the attempt to apply the sympathetic sensations, by formulating rules for the guidance of the student, in performing specific actions for the management of the vocal organs. All three of these topics will be considered in a later chapter. Before approaching this subject let us see just what information may be derived from the observation of the direct sensations of tone.

The direct sensations of tone are never so vivid, so precise, nor so reliable as the sympathetic sensations. In other words, the hearer is better able to judge of the singer's throat action than the singer himself. This may seem a paradoxical statement, but a brief consideration will show it to be fully justified.

In the case of teacher and pupil, it will hardly be questioned that the master hears the pupil's voice to better advantage than the pupil. This is also true when a trained singer's tones are observed by a competent hearer. The singer's direct sensations are highly complex. They include the muscular sensations accompanying the exertion of the breathing muscles, and these are usually so intense as to overshadow the sensations due to the laryngeal adjustments. On the other hand, the hearer is free to pay close attention to the sensations of throat action, and therefore feels these much more keenly than does the singer. On this account the direct sensations of tone are of vastly less value in the study of the vocal action than are the sympathetic sensations.

CHAPTER III

EMPIRICAL KNOWLEDGE OF THE VOICE

Through attention paid to the sympathetic sensations of tone, the listener may carry on mentally a running commentary on the throat actions of all those whose voices are heard. Continuing to use the word empirical in the sense thus far adopted, it may be said that the summary of the impressions conveyed in the sympathetic sensations of tone constitutes empirical knowledge of the voice. In other words, empirical knowledge of the voice is an understanding of the operations of the vocal mechanism, obtained through the attentive listening to voices.

Let us consider first the running commentary on the throat action, mentally carried on by the listener. This mental commentary is an inseparable accompaniment of the listening to the voices of others, whether in speech or song. As we are concerned now only with the problem of tone-production in artistic singing, our consideration will be limited to the critical hearer's observation of the tones of singers.

Let us imagine two friends to be seated side by side in the concert hall, listening to the performance of a violin sonata by an artist of about mediocre ability. Suppose one of the friends to be a highly trained musical critic, the other to be almost unacquainted with music of this class. Let us now inquire how the tones of the violin will impress these two hearers; and further, let the inquiry be limited strictly to the matter of tone, leaving out of consideration all questions of composition and rendition.

As a matter of course, the tones of the violin will impress these two listeners in widely different ways. The untrained observer will greatly enjoy the beautiful tones,--supposing of course that he be gifted with a natural fondness for music. But so far as musical value is concerned, all the tones will sound to him practically alike.

For the trained hearer, on the other hand, every note drawn by the performer from his instrument will have a distinct value. Some of the tones will be true in pitch and perfect in quality. Some will vary slightly from the correct pitch; others will perhaps be in perfect tune, and yet be marred in quality by faults of scratching, thinness, roughness, etc.

When the two come to compare notes at the end of the performance the trained critic will be utterly unable to convey to his friend his impressions of the player's technique. Vividly clear as it is to the critic, his understanding of tonal values is lodged solely in his cultivated ear. This understanding cannot be imparted in words; it must be acquired by experience in actual listening to music.

Let us now imagine this same critic to be listening to a singer, not an artist of the first rank, but one whose voice is marred by some slight faults of production. In this case the critic will note exactly the same sort of differences in tonal value as in the case of the violinist. Some of the singer's notes will be perfect musical tones, others will be marred by faults of intonation or of quality. But a great difference will be noted between faulty tones played on the violin, and faulty tones sung by the human voice. In addition to their blemishes as musical tones, the faulty notes of the voice also convey to the critical listener an idea of the state of the singer's throat in producing them.

Every blemish on the beauty of a vocal tone, every fine shade of quality which detracts from its perfection, indicates to the critical hearer some faulty action of the singer's vocal organs. The more faulty the musical character of the singer's tones the more pronounced is this impression of faulty production. On the other hand, just so nearly as the singer's tones approach perfection as musical sounds, so do they also impress the ear of the critical listener as indicating the approach to the perfect vocal action.

The critic could not impart to his untrained friend the impressions made by the violinist's tones. Somewhat the same is true of the impressions made by the tones of the voice on the critical ear. In voices of extremely nasal or throaty sound these blemishes can, of course, be detected by the ordinary hearer. But the fine shades of difference in vocal tone quality, heard by the trained critic, cannot be noted by the inexperienced listener.

This fine ability to discriminate between musical sounds comes only through experience in listening to music, better still, when this has been combined with the actual study of music. But the ability to judge the vocal actions of singers, through the sympathetic sensations of tone, does not depend on any actual exercise of the listener's own voice. For the developing of this ability the exercise of the ear suffices. The mere exercise of the ear, in listening to singers, entails also the training of what may be called the "mental voice." Attentive listening to voices, involving as a natural consequence the sub-conscious impressions of sympathetic sensations, results in the development of a faculty to which this name, the mental voice, very aptly applies.

A music-lover whose experience of hearing singing and instrumental music has been wide enough to develop the mental voice in a fair degree, possesses in this faculty a valuable means for judging singers. The mental voice carries on a running commentary on the manner of production of all the voices to which this music-lover listens. At every instant he is informed of the exact condition of the singer's throat. For him there is an almost infinite variety of throaty tones, each one indicating some degree and form of throat tension or stiffening. A perfect vocal tone, on the other hand, is felt to be perfectly produced, as well as heard to be musically perfect.

Equipped with a highly trained sense of hearing, and the resulting faculty of mental voice, the lover of singing has an unfailing insight into the operations of the vocal mechanism. This understanding of the workings of the vocal organs is the empirical knowledge of the voice.

This empirical knowledge of the voice can be possessed only by one who is equipped with a highly cultivated ear. The keener the ear the more precise and definite is this understanding of the voice. Season after season, as the music-lover continues to attend concerts, operas, and recitals, his feeling for the voice becomes gradually more keen and discerning.

Further, empirical knowledge of the voice can be acquired in no other way than by actual experience in listening to voices. No matter how keen and definite are the impressions of throat action felt by the experienced hearer, these impressions cannot be described to the uninitiated. In fact, these impressions are to a great extent of a character not capable of being recorded in precise terms. The general nature of a throaty tone, for example, is thoroughly understood. But of the thousands of varieties of the throaty tone no adequate description can be given. Each observer must learn for himself to hear these fine shades of difference in tone quality.

Every experienced music lover has his own mental standard of tonal perfection. The trained ear knows how a perfect musical tone should sound, independent of the precise quality of the tone. The tone quality is determined, of course, by the instrument on which it is sounded. But along with the individual characteristics of the sound, the tones drawn from every instrument, to be available in the artistic performance of music, must conform to the correct standard. Knowing the general musical character of the tones of all instruments, the cultured hearer can at once detect any variation from this character. Further, he knows how the tones of a badly-played instrument would sound if the instrument were correctly handled. An unskilled trumpeter in an orchestra, for example, may draw from his instrument tones that are too brassy, blatant, or harsh. An observant hearer knows exactly what these tones would be if the instrument were skilfully played.

In just the same way the mental voice has its own standard of vocal perfection. Every voice which falls below this standard is felt by the critical hearer to be imperfectly used. When listening to a nasal singer we know that the voice would be greatly improved in quality if the nasal sound of the tones were eliminated. We feel that the correction of the faults of production indicated by a throaty voice would add greatly to the beauty of the voice. More than this, we can also form some idea how an imperfectly produced voice would sound if all the faults of vocal action were to be corrected.

A perfectly produced voice affects the ear in a peculiar and distinct way. Not only is such a voice free from faults; it has also, on the positive side, a peculiar character which renders it entirely different from any wrongly used voice.

The cultured hearer is impressed with a sense of incompleteness and insufficiency in listening to a voice which does not "come out" in a thoroughly satisfactory manner. This is true, even though the voice is not marred by any distinct fault.

A voice absolutely perfect in its production awakens a peculiar set of sympathetic sensations. In addition to its musical beauty such a voice satisfies an instinctive demand for the perfect vocal action. An indescribable sensation of physical satisfaction is experienced in listening to a perfectly managed voice.

On further consideration of this feeling of physical satisfaction awakened by a perfectly produced voice, it seems a mistake to call it indescribable. A beautiful description of this set of sympathetic sensations has been handed down to us by the masters of the old Italian school. This description is embodied in two of the traditional precepts, those dealing with the open throat and the support of the tone.

Mention of the traditional precepts leads at once to the consideration of another aspect of the empirical knowledge of the voice. Vocalists have been attentively listening to voices since the beginning of the modern art of singing. Although many of the impressions made by the voice on the ear cannot be expressed in words, one set of impressions has been clearly recorded. A marked difference was evidently noticed by the old Italian masters between the feelings awakened in the hearer by a voice properly managed and those awakened by an incorrectly produced voice. These impressions were embodied in a set of precepts for the guidance of the singer, which are none other than the much-discussed traditional precepts.

In other words, the traditional precepts embody the results of the old masters' empirical study of the voice. Considered in this light, the old precepts lose at once all air of mystery and become perfectly intelligible and coherent. To a consideration of this record of the empirical knowledge of the voice the following chapter is devoted.

CHAPTER IV

THE TRADITIONAL PRECEPTS OF THE OLD ITALIAN SCHOOL

There should be nothing mysterious, nothing hard to understand, about the empirical precepts. It was pointed out in Chapter V of

Part I that

these precepts contain a perfect description of correctly produced vocal tone, so far as the impression on the listener is concerned. This means nothing else than that the old precepts summarize the results of empirical observation of correct singing. There is nothing new in this statement; considered as empirical knowledge, the modern vocal teacher understands the meaning of the old masters' precepts perfectly well. The misunderstanding of the subject begins with the attempt to apply the precepts as specific rules for the direct mechanical management of the voice. In this connection they were seen to be valueless. Let us now see if the old precepts are found to contain any meaning of value to the vocal teacher when considered as purely empirical formul?

Each one of the precepts may be said to describe some special characteristic of the perfect vocal tone, considered solely as a sound. These characteristics may each be considered separately, that is, the hearer may voluntarily pay close attention to any special aspect of the vocal tone. The best plan for arriving at the exact meaning of the precepts is therefore to consider each one in turn.

The Forward Tone

Every lover of singing is familiar with this characteristic of the perfectly produced voice; the sound seems to come directly from the singer's mouth, and gives no indication of being formed at the back of the throat. This characteristic of the perfect tone is simply heard. It is not distinguished by any sympathetic sensations, but is purely a matter of sound. On the other hand, a wrongly produced voice seems to be formed or held in the back of the singer's throat. The tones of such a voice do not come out satisfactorily; they seem to be lodged in the throat instead of at the front of the mouth.

In the badly used voice the impression of throat is conveyed by the sympathetic sensations awakened in the hearer. A striking difference between correct and incorrect singing is thus noted. A wrongly produced voice is felt by the hearer to be held in the singer's throat. When properly used the voice gives no impression of throat; it seems to have no relation to the throat, but to be formed in the front of the mouth.

So much has been written about "forward emission" that the forward characteristic of vocal tones seems to be enshrouded in mystery. As a matter of fact, the forward tone is easily explained. The perfectly produced voice issues directly from the mouth for the same reason that the tones of the trombone issue from the bell of the instrument. It is all a matter of resonance. This is well illustrated by a simple experiment with a tuning fork and a spherical resonator reinforcing the tone of the fork.

When the fork is struck, the ear hears the sound issuing from the resonator, not that coming direct from the fork. This is brought out distinctly by placing the fork at a little distance from the resonator. The listener can then definitely locate the source of the sound which impresses the ear. Under these circumstances the sound coming from the resonator is found to be many times more powerful than that coming direct from the tuning fork. If left to its own judgment the ear takes the resonator to be the original source of the sound.

In the voice the exciting cause of the air vibrations is located at the back of the resonator,--the mouth-pharynx cavity. The sound waves in this case can issue only from the front of the resonator,--the singer's mouth. No matter how the voice is produced, correctly or badly, this acoustic principle must apply.

Why then does not the incorrectly used voice impress the hearer as issuing directly from the mouth, the same as the correctly produced tone? This is purely a matter of sympathetic sensations of throat tightness, awakened by the faulty tone. Every wrongly used voice arouses in the listener sympathetic sensations of throat contraction. This impression of throat, noted by the hearer, consists of muscular, not of strictly auditory sensations.

As a statement of scientific fact, the forward-tone precept is erroneous. It does not describe scientifically the difference between correct and incorrect tone-production. Correctly sung tones are not produced at the lips. Every vocal tone, good or bad, is produced by the motion of the vocal cords and reinforced by the resonance of the mouth-pharynx cavity. Only when considered as an empirical description is the forward-tone precept of value. In this sense the precept describes accurately the difference in the impressions made on the hearer by correct and incorrect singing. A badly produced tone seems to be caught in the singer's throat; the correctly used voice is free from this fault, and is therefore heard to issue directly from the singer's mouth.

This marked difference between correct and incorrect tone throws a valuable light on the meaning of the correct vocal action. Every badly used voice gives the impression of wrong or unnecessary tightness, stiffening, and contraction of the throat. When perfectly used, the voice does not convey any such impression of throat stiffness.

The Open Throat

Just as with the forward tone, the meaning of the open throat is best brought out by contrasting the impressions made on the hearer by a perfect and a badly used voice. A badly produced tone seems to be caught, or as Tosi expressed it, "choaked in the throat." The singer's throat seems to be tightened and narrowed so that the sound has not sufficient passageway to come out properly. On the other hand, the perfectly used voice comes out freely, without interference or hindrance at any point in the singer's throat. There seems to be plenty of room for the tone to come forth; in other words, the singer's throat seems to be open.

All these impressions are purely a matter of sympathetic sensations. In listening to a faulty singer the hearer feels a sensation of tightness and contraction of the throat. A well used voice awakens exactly the opposite sensation, that of looseness and freedom of the throat.

Here again is seen the difference between correct and incorrect singing, empirically considered. Judging from the impressions made by rightly and wrongly used voices, any incorrect vocal action involves a condition of tightness and contraction of the throat. Perfect singing gives the impression that the throat is loose and supple, and free from all unnecessary tension.

The Support of the Tone

Following the plan of contrasting correct and incorrect singing, the meaning of this precept is readily found. The perfect voice is felt by the hearer to be firmly and confidently held by the singer in a secure grasp of the throat muscles. Such a voice awakens the sympathetic sensations of perfectly balanced muscular effect, similar to the muscular sensations of the hand and forearm when an object is firmly grasped in the hand.

A badly used voice seems to be convulsively gripped in the singer's throat. The tones seem to fall back into the throat for want of some secure base on which to rest. This impression is conveyed by a peculiar set of sympathetic sensations of highly unpleasant muscular tension far back in the throat.

This precept, "Support the tone," points to the difference already noted between the right and the wrong vocal action. Badly produced tones indicate a state of excessive tension of the throat muscles. Correct singing gives the impression that the throat muscles exert exactly the requisite degree of strength, and no more.

Taken together, the open-throat and the forward-tone precepts embody an admirable description of the sympathetic sensations awakened by perfect singing. The singer's entire vocal mechanism is felt to be in a condition of lithe and supple freedom. There is no straining, no constraint, no forcing, no unnecessary tension. Each muscle of the vocal mechanism, and indeed of the entire body, exerts just the necessary degree of strength.

Similar muscular sensations always accompany the expert performance of any action requiring a high degree of dexterity. Whatever be the form of exertion, skilful physical activity awakens muscular sensations of perfectly balanced and harmonized contractions. This feeling of muscular poise and adjustment is pleasurable in a high degree.

A keen enjoyment is experienced in the skilful performance of many complex muscular activities. Much of the pleasure of skating, dancing, rowing, tennis, etc., is dependent on this feeling of muscular poise and harmonious contraction. Healthy exercise is always normally enjoyable; but skilful performance greatly enhances the pleasure. A beginner learning to skate, for example, exerts himself fully as much as the accomplished skater. Yet the beginner does not by any means derive the same degree of pleasure from his exertions.

Precisely this feeling of balanced and harmonious muscular exertion is experienced by the perfect singer. More than this, the hearer also, through sympathetic sensations, shares the same pleasurable feeling. This is the sensation described as the feeling of soaring, of poise, and of floating, in many descriptions of the "singer's sensations."

Singing on the Breath

When the voice is perfectly used the tones seem to detach themselves from the singer, and to float off on the breath. Nothing in the sound of the tones, nor in the sympathetic sensations awakened, gives any indication that the breath is checked or impeded in its flow. The current of tone seems to be poured out on the breath just as freely as a quiet expiration in ordinary breathing.

This is a purely empirical description of perfect singing. As we know very well, the vocal action is quite different from this description. But the important point is that the phrase "singing on the breath" does very accurately describe the impression made on the hearer by perfect singing.

Singing on the breath represents the highest possible degree of purely vocal perfection. One may attend operas and concerts for a whole season and listen to a score of famous singers, and count oneself fortunate to have heard even one artist who attains this standard of tonal excellence. Singing on the breath is an effect of wondrous tonal beauty; it is simply this, pure beauty, pristine and na 風習 e.

With the slightest degree of throat stiffness or muscular tension, singing on the breath is utterly impossible. So soon as the tones indicate the merest trace of throat contraction, the free outflow of the stream of sound is felt to be checked.

Coloratura singing, to be absolutely perfect, demands this degree of tonal excellence. Singing on the breath and coloratura are indeed very closely allied.

The modern school of musical criticism does not hold coloratura singing in very high esteem. We demand nowadays expression, passion, and emotion; we want vocal music to portray definite sentiments, to express concrete feelings. Florid singing is not adapted to this form of expressiveness. It is only sensuously beautiful; it speaks to the ear, but does not appeal to the intellect.

Yet it may well be asked whether the highest type of coloratura singing, pure tonal beauty, does not appeal to a deeper, more elemental set of emotions than are reached by dramatically expressive singing. This question would call for a profound psychological discussion, hardly in place in a work devoted to the technical problem of tone-production. But this much is certain: Coloratura singing still has a strong hold on the affections of the music loving public. Even to-day audiences are moved by the vocal feats of some famous queen of song fully as profoundly as by the performance of a modern dramatic or realistic opera.

To describe a sound is an extremely difficult task. The tone of the muted horn, for example, is perfectly familiar to the average musician. Yet who would undertake to describe in words the tone of the muted horn? A description of the sounds produced by a perfectly managed voice is almost as difficult to frame in words. Still the old Italian masters succeeded in finding words to describe perfect singing. These few simple phrases--open the throat, support the tone, sing the tones forward, sing on the breath--embody a most beautiful and complete description of vocal perfection. The empirical study of the voice can hardly be expected to go further than this. From the old masters we have received a complete record of all that need be known empirically about the voice.

CHAPTER V

EMPIRICAL KNOWLEDGE IN MODERN VOICE CULTURE

It was pointed out in Chapter I of

Part III that there is no possibility

of conflict between empirical and scientific knowledge. Modern Voice Culture seems to present a direct contradiction of this statement. The vocal teacher's empirical understanding of the voice conflicts at every step with his supposedly scientific knowledge. No doubt the reader is already aware of the real meaning of this apparent contradiction. It only bears out the philosophic rule; an accepted science must be abandoned so soon as its deductions are found to be not in accord with observed facts.

Modern methods of instruction in singing can be understood only by following out this idea of conflict between known facts and accepted, though erroneous, scientific doctrines. As we have seen, the only universally accepted theory of supposedly scientific Voice Culture is the idea of direct mechanical guidance of the voice. Every vocal teacher attempts to make his empirical knowledge conform to this mechanical idea. As the empirical knowledge is correct, and the mechanical idea a complete mistake, conflict between the two is inevitable.

Every modern teacher of singing possesses in full measure the empirical understanding of the voice. To this statement hardly an exception need be made. Probably the most startling fact concerning the wide diffusion of this knowledge is that the nature of this knowledge is so thoroughly ignored. Because the psychological process is purely sub-conscious, empirical knowledge is always indirectly and generally unconsciously applied. In the teacher's mind the most prominent idea is that of mechanical vocal guidance. His attention is always directly turned to this idea. Empirical knowledge, consisting merely of a succession of auditory and muscular sensations, lurks in the background of consciousness.

To the intelligent vocal teacher there is something peculiarly fascinating about the study of tone-production. In listening to any faulty singer we feel with the utmost precision what is wrong with the voice. Each imperfect tone informs us clearly and definitely just where the wrong muscular contraction is located. It seems so easy to tell the singer what to do in order to bring the tone out perfectly. Under the influence of the mechanical idea we try to express this feeling in the terms of muscular action. This attempt is never successful; the singer cannot be brought to understand our meaning. Yet it is so clear in our own minds that our inability to express it is extremely tantalizing. We go on, constantly hoping to find a way to define the mechanical processes so clearly indicated to the ear. We always feel that we are just on the verge of the great discovery. The solution of the problem of tone-production is almost within our grasp, yet it always eludes us.

It was stated in Chapter V of

Part I that empirical knowledge of the

voice, based on the singer's sensations, is used to supplement and interpret the doctrines of mechanical vocal guidance. This is in the main true, so far as the vocal teacher is aware. But here again the result of the sub-conscious character of empirical knowledge of the voice is seen. As a matter of fact the real situation is the direct reverse of that described in the chapter mentioned. The mechanical doctrines are used in the attempt to interpret the empirical knowledge. This fact is well brought out in the following passage from Kofler: "The teacher must imitate the wrong muscle-action and tone of his pupil as an illustration of the negative side." (The Art of Breathing, N. Y., 1889.) Kofler does not touch on the question, how the teacher is able to locate the wrong muscle-action of the pupil. He takes this ability for granted; it is so purely an intuitive process that he does not stop to inquire into the source of this information of the pupil's vocal action. Through his sense of hearing he sub-consciously locates the faults in the pupil's tone-production. His only conscious application of this knowledge is the attempt to explain to the pupil the wrong muscle-action. This he naturally tries to do in the terms of mechanical action and muscular operation. Thus the mechanical doctrine is used in the attempt to explain the empirical knowledge. Yet the teacher is conscious only of citing the mechanical rule, and believes this to cover the entire instruction.

In the preceding chapter it was seen that the perfectly produced vocal tone may be considered in a variety of aspects. Each one of these aspects is characterized by a fairly distinct set of sympathetic sensations. Of faulty modes of throat action, as revealed by sympathetic sensations, there is an almost infinite variety. Of this wide variety of forms of throat tension the most prominent are those indicated by sets of sympathetic sensations, the direct opposites of those characterizing the perfect vocal action. Thus the open throat is indicated by one set of sympathetic sensations, the lack of this characteristic of tone by an opposite set, etc.

Whatever distinct fault of production the pupil's tone indicates, the master immediately notes the character of the faulty throat action. The master feels, simply and directly, what is wrong with the student's tone-production. Whence this knowledge comes he does not stop to inquire. Suppose the pupil to sing an exercise, and to produce tones which stick in the throat, instead of coming out freely. The master simply hears that the pupil's voice is caught in the throat; he does not observe that he is informed of this condition by muscular as well as auditory sensations.

This ignoring of the psychological nature of the impressions of tone is not necessarily detrimental to successful instruction. On the contrary, the master's empirical insight into the vocal operations of the pupil would probably not be advanced by an understanding of the psychological process. It is sufficient for the teacher's purpose to hear that the pupil's voice is caught in the throat. What robs this hearing, or feeling, of all value is this: the master attempts to interpret the sensation as an indication of the need of some specific muscular action, to be directly performed by the pupil. To this end he cites the mechanical rule, assumed to be indicated by the pupil's faulty vocal action. This may be, for example, the opening of the throat to give room for the tone to expand. It seems so perfectly simple to the teacher;--the pupil narrows his throat, and so holds in the tone; let him expand his throat and the tone will come out freely. This conclusion seems so clearly indicated by the sound of the tones that the master almost inevitably gives the precise instruction: "Open your throat and let your voice come out." This sums up, to the master's satisfaction, everything the pupil need do to correct this particular fault of tone-production.

Other sets of sympathetic sensations, awakened by badly produced tones, are interpreted in the same manner. A tone heard to be held in the back of the throat is believed to indicate the need of bringing the voice forward in the mouth. Other forms of throaty production are taken to show a lack of support, a wrong management of the breath, a need of breath-control, a misuse of nasal resonance, or an improper action of the vocal cords. In all these attempts to interpret sympathetic sensations by means of mechanical doctrines the teacher naturally relies on those doctrines in which he believes most firmly. Sympathetic sensations are indeed sometimes cited in proof of certain theories of breath-control, and also of nasal resonance. Both these topics are worthy of separate attention.

Sympathetic Sensations and Nasal Resonance

One of the most widely accepted theories of the vocal action is that the higher notes of the voice are influenced by reinforcing vibrations located in the nose and forehead. Whether this idea was derived more from direct than from sympathetic sensations need not be determined now. It is at any rate certain that a perfectly sung tone gives to the hearer the impression of nasal influence of some kind. The exact nature of this influence has never been determined. It may be air resonance, or sounding-board resonance, or both combined. Satisfactory proof on this point is lacking. In the belief of the practical teacher, however, this impression of nasal influence is the strongest argument in favor of nasal resonance.

Turning now to the question of nasal quality, strictly speaking, tones of this objectionable character always awaken the sympathetic sensations of contraction somewhere in the nose. Why such a contraction should cause this unpleasant sound of the voice is a profound mystery. Perhaps wrong tension of the soft palate exerts an influence on the actions of the vocal cords; or it may be that the form of the nasal cavities is altered by the muscular contraction. This aspect of the vocal action has never been scientifically investigated. The sympathetic sensation of nasal contraction or pinching is at any rate very pronounced. Curiously, this sympathetic sensation is cited as an argument in favor of their respective theories, by both the advocates and the opponents of nasal resonance.

Sympathetic Sensations and Breath-Control

Certain forms of exaggerated throat stiffness are frequently held to indicate the need of breath-control. The faulty vocal action in question is analyzed by the breath-control advocates substantially as follows: "Owing to the outflow of the breath not being checked at the proper point, the entire vocal mechanism is thrown out of adjustment. The singer exerts most of his efforts in the endeavor to prevent the escape of the breath; to this end he contracts his throat and stiffens his tongue and jaw. His tones are forced, harsh, and breathy; they lack musical quality. His voice runs away with him and he cannot control or manage it. In the attempt to obtain some hold on his voice he 'reaches' for his tones with his throat muscles. The more he tries to regain control of the runaway breath the worse does his state become."

This extreme condition of throat stiffness is unfortunately by no means rare. So far as concerns the sympathetic sensations awakened by this kind of singing the condition is graphically described by the breath-control advocates. But the conclusion is entirely unjustified that this condition indicates the lack of breath-control. Only the preconceived notion of breath-control leads to this inference. The sympathetic sensations indicate a state of extreme muscular tension of the throat; this is about the only possible analysis of the condition.

* * *

Empirical impressions of vocal tones determine the character of most present-day instruction in singing. This means no more than to say that throughout all vocal training the teacher listens to the pupil's voice. The impressions of tone received by the teacher's ear cannot fail to inform the teacher of the condition of the pupil's throat in producing the voice. For the teacher to seek to apply this information in imparting the correct vocal action to the pupil is inevitable.

Almost every teacher begins a course of instruction by having the pupil run through the prescribed series of mechanical exercises and rules. Breathing is always taken up first. Breath-control, laryngeal action, registers, and resonance follow usually in this order. The time devoted to this course of training may vary from a few weeks to several months. This mechanical instruction is almost always interspersed with songs and arias. The usual procedure is to devote about half of each lesson to mechanical doctrines and the remainder to real singing.

Blind faith in the efficacy of this mechanical training is the teacher's only motive in giving it. Very little attention is paid to the sound of the pupil's voice during the study of mechanical rules and doctrines. It is simply taken for granted that the voice must be put through this course. Once the mechanical course has been covered, the pupil's voice is supposed, in a vague way, to be "placed." From that time on, whether it be at the end of two months of study or of two years, the instruction is based solely on empirical impressions of tone.

Little remains to be said of the nature of this empirical instruction. It always retains the mechanical aspect. Whatever fault of production is noted, the teacher seeks to correct the fault by applying some mechanical rule. The futility of this form of instruction has already been pointed out.

Only two ways of applying empirical knowledge of the voice are known to the modern vocal teacher. These are, first, to tell the pupil to "open the throat," or to "support the tone," or to perform whatever other mechanical operation seems to be indicated as necessary by the sound of the tone; second, to bid the student to "feel that the tone is supported," to "feel that the throat is open," etc. Under these circumstances the little advantage derived from empirical knowledge in modern Voice Culture is readily understood.

CHAPTER VI

SCIENTIFIC KNOWLEDGE OF THE VOICE

So far as any definite record can be made, the knowledge of the voice obtained by attentive listening to voices has now been set down. The next step in the scientific study of tone-production is the consideration of all knowledge of the voice obtained from sources other than empirical. In other words, the knowledge of the voice usually classed as scientific is now to be examined.

Three sciences are generally held to contribute all that can possibly be known about the vocal action. These are anatomy, acoustics, and mechanics. Of these anatomy has received by far the most attention from vocal scientists. The laws of acoustics, bearing on the voice, have also been carefully considered. Beyond the theory of breath-control, little attempt has been made to apply the principles of mechanics in Vocal Science. Psychology, the science most intimately concerned with the management of the voice, has received almost no attention in this connection.

A complete record of the teachings of the established sciences with regard to the voice demands the separate consideration of the four sciences mentioned. Each will therefore be treated in turn. In the case of each of these sciences it is seen that the most essential facts of the vocal action have been definitely established. Many questions still remain to be satisfactorily answered which are of great interest to the theoretical student of the voice. Yet in spite of the lack of exact knowledge on these points, enough is now known to furnish the basis for a practical science of Voice Culture.

The Anatomy of the Vocal Mechanism

This subject has been so exhaustively studied that nothing new can well be discovered regarding the muscular structure of the vocal organs. In all probability the reader is sufficiently acquainted with the anatomy of the larynx and its connections. Only a very brief outline of the subject is therefore demanded. The muscles concerned with breathing call for no special notice in this connection.

The special organ of voice is the larynx. This consists of four cartilages, with their connecting ligaments,--the thyroid, the cricoid, and the two arytenoids, and of nine so-called intrinsic muscles,--two crico-thyroid, right and left, two thyro-arytenoid, two posterior crico-arytenoid, two lateral crico-arytenoid, and one arytenoideus. The inner edges of the thyro-arytenoid muscles form the vocal cords. The hyoid bone, serving as a medium of attachment for the tongue, may also be considered a portion of the larynx. By means of the extrinsic muscles the larynx is connected with the bones of the chest, neck, and head.

While the muscular structure of the vocal organs is thoroughly known, the actions of the laryngeal muscles in tone-production have never been absolutely determined. This much is definitely established: Vocal tone is produced when the vocal cords are brought together and held on tension, and the air in the lungs is expired with sufficient force to set the vocal cords in motion. The tension of the vocal cords can be increased by the contraction of their muscular tissues, the two thyro-arytenoid muscles; further, increased tension of the cords can also result from the tilting of the thyroid cartilage on the cricoid, by the contraction of the crico-thyroid muscles.

It is also definitely proved that the pitch of the vocal tone varies with the state of tension of the vocal cords; increasing the degree of tension raises the pitch, decreasing the tension lowers it. As to the relative importance of the different groups of muscles in varying the tension of the vocal cords, nothing has been definitely proved.

In addition to the variations in pitch resulting from variations in the tension of the vocal cords, there is also much ground for believing that the pitch may be raised by shortening the effective length of the vocal cords. This is apparently accomplished by the rotation of the arytenoid cartilages; but the specific muscular contractions concerned in the rotation of the arytenoids have not been located.

It is generally asserted by vocal theorists that the quality of the vocal tone, on any one note, is determined mainly by the influence of the resonance cavities. Dr. Mills says on this point: "When it is borne in mind that the vocal bands have little or nothing to do with the quality of the tone, the importance of those parts of the vocal apparatus which determine quality... becomes apparent." (Voice Production in Singing and Speaking, 1906.) This theory that the quality of the tone is determined solely by the resonance cavities is directly contradicted by Prof. Scripture. He proves that changes in tone quality result from changes in vocal cord adjustment. This subject is more fully treated in the following section. Even before this matter had been definitely settled by Prof. Scripture, there was a strong presumption in favor of the vocal cord adjustment theory. Howard advanced this idea in 1883. Several empirical observations support this theory. Most important of these is the fact that a single tone, swelled from piano to forte, goes through a wide variety of changes in quality. Stockhausen's mention of this fact has already been noted.

This fact tends to cast some doubt on the value of laryngoscopic observation as a means of determining the laryngeal action. Under the conditions necessary for examination with the laryngoscope it is impossible for the singer to produce any but soft tones in the head quality of voice. Most of these tones, if swelled to forte, would change from the head to the chest quality. It is probable that this change in quality is effected by a corresponding change in the vocal cord adjustment, as the conditions of the resonance cavities remain the same. But this cannot be determined by laryngoscopic observation.

So far as the actions of the laryngeal muscles are concerned, no difference can be defined between the correct vocal action and any improper mode of operation. Sir Morell Mackenzie examined a large number of people with the aid of the laryngoscope; of these, some were trained singers, others, while possessed of good natural voices, had had no vocal training whatever. Many variations were noted in the notes on which changes of register occurred. But it could not be determined by this mode of examination whether the subject was a trained singer or not.

If there is one specifically correct mode of operation for the vocal cords, this correct action has never been determined from the anatomy of the organs. No doubt there is some difference between the muscular actions of correct tone-production and those of any incorrect operation of the voice. But the nature of this difference in muscular action has never been discovered by means of dissections of the larynx, nor by laryngoscopic observation.

The Acoustic Principles of Tone-Production

An outline of the existing state of knowledge regarding the acoustic principles of tone-production must be drawn mainly from one source. This is the latest authoritative work on the subject, The Study of Speech Curves, by E. W. Scripture (Washington, 1906). In this work Prof. Scripture overthrows several of the conclusions of Helmholtz which had hitherto furnished the basis of all the accepted theories of vocal acoustics. Considering the eminently scientific character of all Prof. Scripture's research work, his thorough acquaintance with every detail of the subject, and the exhaustive attention devoted to this series of experiments, we are fully justified in accepting his present statements as conclusively proved.

A first impression received from a careful reading of The Study of Speech Curves is that the subject is vastly more intricate than had formerly been believed. Helmholtz's theory of vocal acoustics was fairly simple: The vocal cords vibrate after the manner of membranous reeds; a tone thus produced consists of a fundamental and a series of overtones; vowel and tone quality are determined by the influence of the resonance cavities, which reinforce certain of the overtones with special prominence. This theory is discarded by Prof. Scripture. "The overtone theory of the vowels cannot be correct." In place of this simple theory, Prof. Scripture reaches conclusions too complicated to be given in detail here. A brief outline of the subject must suffice for the needs of the present work.

Prof. Scripture found that the nature of the walls of a resonating cavity is of more importance than either its size, shape, or opening. A flesh-lined cavity is capable of reinforcing tones covering a range of several notes. Further, the vowel sound, and presumably also the tone quality, are determined more by the action of the vocal cords than by the adjustment of the resonance cavities. "The glottal lips vibrate differently for the different vowels." This adjustment of the glottal lips "presumably occurs by nervously aroused contractions of the fibers of the muscles in the glottal lips." Continuing, Prof. Scripture says:

"Physiologically stated, the action for a vowel is as follows: Each glottal lip consists mainly of a mass of muscles supported at the ends and along the lateral side. It bears no resemblance to a membrane or a string. The two lips come together at their front ends, but diverge to the rear. The rear ends are attached to the arytenoid cartilages. When the ends are brought together by rotation of these arytenoid cartilages, the medial surfaces touch. At the same time they are stretched by the action of the crico-thyroid muscles, which pull apart the points of support at the ends.

"In this way the two masses of muscle close the air passage. To produce a vowel such a relation of air pressure and glottal tension is arranged that the air from the trachea bursts the muscles apart for a moment, after which they close again; the release of the puff of air reduces the pressure in the trachea and they remain closed until the pressure is again sufficient to burst them apart. With appropriate adjustments of the laryngeal muscles and air pressure this is kept up indefinitely, and a series of puffs from the larynx is produced. The glottal lips open partly by yielding sidewise,--that is, they are compressed,--and partly by being shoved upward and outward. The form of the puff, sharp or smooth, is determined by the way in which the glottal lips yield; the mode of yielding depends on the way in which the separate fibers of the muscles are contracted.

"These puffs act on the vocal cavity, that is, on a complicated system of cavities (trachea, larynx, pharynx, mouth, nose) with variable shapes, sizes, and openings. The effect of the puffs on each element of the vocal cavity is double: first, to arouse in it a vibration with a period depending on the cavity; second, to force on it a vibration of the same period as that of the set of puffs. The prevalence of one of the factors over the other depends on the form of the puff, the walls of the cavities, etc."

Prof. Scripture does not undertake to point out a difference between the correct vocal action in tone-production, and any incorrect action. This difference in action does not seem capable of definition by any analysis of the acoustic principles involved.

Mechanical Principles of the Vocal Action

In

Part II, Chapter II, it was seen that the outflow of the breath in

tone-production is checked by the vocal cords, in accordance with Pascal's law of fluid pressures. Another law of mechanics bearing on this operation is now to be considered, viz., the law of the transformation and conservation of energy.

The application of the law of the transformation and conservation of energy to the operations of the voice is nicely illustrated by the well-known candle-flame test of (supposedly) breath-control. To perform this test the singer is instructed to practise the exercises for breath-control while holding a lighted candle with the flame an inch or two in front of the lips. According to the idea of the breath-control advocates, the expired breath should escape so slowly, and with so little force, that no current of air can be detected at the lips, the expiration therefore does not cause the candle flame to flicker.

Describing the toneless breathing exercises to be practised with the candle flame, Browne and Behnke say, "Let it be observed that the above exercise is quite distinct from the well-known practice of singing before a lighted candle, which is, comparatively speaking, an easy matter." (Voice, Song, and Speech.) A very striking fact is stated correctly by Browne and Behnke,--there is no current of air created at the lips during tone-production. Of the truth of this statement the reader may readily convince himself by trying this same experiment with a candle flame, or even with a lighted match. Hold a lighted match just in front of the lips and sing a powerful tone. The quality of the tone is of no consequence so long as it be powerful. Just sing, shout, yell, the louder the better. You will find that the flame is less affected under these circumstances than by the quiet expiration of ordinary breathing.

Considerable practice and close attention are required in order to hold back the breath in toneless breathing exercises. Whereas in producing any kind of powerful tone the breath normally creates no current of air at the lips.

There is no reason for considering this experiment a test of correct tone-production. It is impossible to produce a powerful tone of any kind, good, bad, or indifferent, and at the same time to create an appreciable current of air at the lips.

Needless to say, the breath-control theorists have entirely failed to grasp the significance of the candle-flame experiment. Yet we have here a demonstration of the mechanical law of tone-production.

Considered as a mechanical process, tone-production occurs when the energy exerted by the expiratory muscles, in their contraction, is converted into energy of motion of the vocal cords.[8] In other words, tone-production is an example of the transformation of energy. The law of the transformation and conservation of energy must therefore apply to this operation. This law is stated as follows: "Energy may be transformed from any of its forms to any other form. When energy is thus transformed the quantity of energy in the resulting form or forms is equal to the quantity of energy in the original form."

[Note 8: This exposition of the mechanical principle of tone-production is intended to be graphic, rather than strictly technical. For the sake of simplicity, that portion of the expiratory energy expended in friction against the throat walls, tongue, cheeks, etc., is disregarded, as well as that expended in propelling the air out of the mouth, in displacing the same quantity of external air, etc.]

The mechanical operation of tone-production comprises the following transformations of energy: First, the energy exerted in the contraction of the expiratory muscles is converted into energy of condensation or elasticity of the air in the lungs and trachea. Second, this energy of condensation of the air is converted into energy of motion of the vocal cords. In other words, the expiratory energy is transformed into energy of motion.

One objection, at first sight very serious, may be offered against this statement: the amount of strength exerted in the contractions of the breath muscles seems many times greater than is accounted for in the motion of the vocal cords. The movements of the vocal cords are so slight as to be observable only with the aid of a specially devised apparatus, the stroboscope. Can all the expiratory force expended in tone-production show such a small result? This apparent objection is found to be groundless in view of the application in this operation of Pascal's law. As this topic was fully treated in Chapter II of

Part II,

no further explanation is required here.

The erroneous idea of vocal mechanics involved in the doctrine of breath-control is now fully exposed. Tone can be produced only when the expired air exerts a pressure on the vocal cords. There is no necessity for any conscious or voluntary check on the expiration. The energy of the expiration is expended in setting the vocal cords in motion. No energy of condensation is left in the expired air the instant it has passed the vocal cords. Beyond that point there is no expiratory pressure.

In one sense it is true that the expiration is "controlled" in tone-production. But this control is strictly an automatic action. The vocal cords are adjusted, by the appropriate muscular contractions, to move in response to the air pressure exerted against them. This action involves, as a necessary consequence, the holding back by the vocal cords of the out-rushing air. So long as the vocal cords remain in the position for producing tone, they also control the expiration. In this sense breath-control is an inseparable feature of tone-production.

All that need be known of the mechanics of the voice is therefore perfectly plain. The vocal cords are set in motion by the pressure against them of the expired breath. This operation is in accordance with Pascal's law and the law of the conservation of energy.

But this analysis throws no light on the nature of the correct vocal action. It is impossible for the voice to produce a sound in any way other than that just described. In speaking or in singing, in laughing or in crying, in every sound produced by the action of the vocal cords, the mechanical principle is always the same. Nor is the bearing of this law limited to the human voice. Every singing bird, every animal whose vocal mechanism consists of lungs and larynx, illustrates the same mechanical principle of vocal action.

Only passing mention is required of the fallacy of the breath-band theory. The idea of any necessity of relieving the vocal cords of the expiratory pressure is purely fanciful. How any one with even a slight understanding of mechanics could imagine the checking of the breath by the inflation of the ventricles of Morgagni, is hard to conceive.

The Psychology of Tone-Production

This subject was treated, in some detail, in Chapter V of

Part II. In

that chapter however we were concerned more with a destructive criticism of the idea of mechanical tone-production than with the positive features of vocal psychology. At the risk of some repetition it is therefore advisable here to sum up the laws of psychology bearing on the vocal action.

Considered as a psychological process, tone-production in singing involves three distinct operations. First, the mental ear conceives a tone of definite pitch, quality, vowel sound, and power. Second, the vocal organs prepare to adjust themselves, by the appropriate muscular contractions, for the production of the tone mentally conceived. Third, the fiat of will is issued, causing the muscular contractions to be performed. These three operations are executed as one conscious, voluntary act. Let us inquire to what extent consciousness is concerned with each operation.

As conscious volitional impulses, the mental conception of the tone, and the fiat of will to produce the tone, are well enough understood. These two operations call for no extended consideration. We are at present concerned only with the psychological laws bearing on the muscular adjustments of the vocal organs.

Muscular contractions result from the transmission to the muscular fibers of motor nerve impulses. These nerve impulses originate in the motor nerve centers. They can never, under any circumstances, rise into consciousness. Contractions of the voluntary muscles occur either as reflex or as voluntary actions. In both cases the motor nerve impulses originate in the same nerve centers. In the case of reflex actions these lower muscular centers alone are involved; in voluntary actions the originating of the motor impulses is "controlled" by consciousness. In deciding that an action shall be performed, and in what way it is to be performed, consciousness directs that each motor center involved shall send out the appropriate discharges of nerve impulse.

Complex muscular activities require the sending out of nerve impulses from various motor centers. Such activities are usually not performed instantaneously, but require a longer or shorter time. Thus we may consider it as one action for the writer to rise from his chair, to lower the window and adjust the shade, and then to return to his seat. In this case a large number of motor centers are successively involved; at the proper instant each center discharges its impulse. To this end the motor centers must be instructed when to come into activity.

This distribution of nerve impulse is effected by the power of coordination. In voluntary actions coordination is accompanied by conscious control.[9] But coordination is not a function of the higher cerebral centers, that is, of consciousness. How the connection is made between the higher cerebral centers and the lower motor centers is a complete mystery. All that can be said is that the ideas of movements are transmitted to the motor centers, and that these send out the appropriate motor impulses.

[Note 9: In this connection it is advisable to point out a difference between the meanings attached to the word "control" in psychology and in Vocal Science. The psychologist classes habitual movements as either automatic or controlled. Automatic movements are purely reflex; the individual does not consciously decide whether they shall be performed or not. Psychologically considered, the control of a movement is simply the conscious volitional decision whether the movement shall be performed. To adopt the language of Psychology, we should speak of voice management, and of breath regulation, instead of vocal control, breath control, etc. In the following chapters the accepted psychological usage of the word "control" will so far as possible be adopted.]

Turning now to the muscular adjustments of the vocal organs, these adjustments are seen to be independent of conscious guidance. When a tone is mentally conceived the vocal organs adjust themselves, in response to some mysterious guidance, for the production of the tone. The vocal cords assume the appropriate degree of tension according to the pitch of the tone to be sung. Both the quality of the tone and the vowel are determined by the combined adjustments of the laryngeal muscles and of the muscles which fix the shape and size of the resonance cavities. The power of the tone is regulated by the force of the breath blast; for each degree of power some special adjustment of the vocal cords is required.

All these adjustments are executed as one concrete and individual act in response to the volitional impulse contained in the mental conception of the tone. The tone is conceived as a concrete whole. It is not normally broken up mentally into its four aspects of pitch, quality, vowel, and power. True, each one of these four characteristics of the tone may be separately considered by the singer. So also, to a certain extent, may the adjustments of the vocal organs be performed with special reference to one or the other characteristic of the tone. But in every case the muscular contractions are performed without direct conscious guidance. Whatever be the character of the tone mentally demanded, the vocal organs instantly adjust themselves to produce the tone.

What is meant by saying that the muscular contractions are performed without conscious guidance? Does this mean that the singer is unconscious of the muscular contractions? Not at all. Muscular sense informs the singer, more or less distinctly, of the state of contraction or relaxation of the various muscles of the vocal organs. The singer always knows fairly well the condition of the various parts of the vocal mechanism. What is meant is this: The singer does not consciously direct the vocal organs to assume certain positions and conditions, and does not instruct the various muscles to contract in certain ways. The singer does not need to know, and in fact cannot know, what muscular contractions are required to produce any desired tone.

Some connection exists between the organs of hearing and the vocal mechanism. That this connection has a physical basis in the nervous structure is fairly well established. "The centers for sight and for arm movements, for instance, or those of hearing and of vocal movements, have connecting pathways between them." (Feeling and Will, Jas. M. Baldwin, 1894.) The psychological law of tone-production is that the vocal organs adjust themselves, without conscious guidance, to produce the tones mentally conceived. In actual singing the practical application of this law is that the voice is guided by the ear.

This guidance of the voice by the ear is incessant. It must not be understood that the mental ear simply conceives a single tone, and that the vocal machinery then operates without further guidance. All the characteristics of the vocal tones,--pitch, quality, and power,--are constantly changing. These changes require corresponding changes in the muscular adjustments. The muscular contractions in turn are guided by the demands of the mental ear. As a psychological process, singing may therefore be analyzed as follows: The singer mentally sings the composition. In response to the ever varying demands of the ear the vocal organs adjust themselves to produce actually the sounds thus mentally conceived. The singer listens to these sounds and at every instant compares them to the mental conception. If the tones actually produced fail to correspond exactly to those mentally conceived, the singer instantly notes this variation and bids the vocal organs to correct it. The ear has therefore a dual function in singing. First, the mental ear directs the voice in its operations. Second, the physical ear acts as a check or corrective on the voice.

To sum up the psychology of tone-production, the singer guides or manages the voice by attentively listening to the tones of the voice. This is the only possible means of vocal guidance. The voice and the ear together form one complete organ.

But we are still apparently as far as ever from the specific meaning of the correct vocal action. That the voice instinctively obeys the commands of the ear may be true theoretically. In actual practice we know that this does not by any means always occur. Singers are often unable to get the desired results from their voices, even when they believe themselves to rely on the sense of hearing. There must therefore be some influence which under certain conditions interferes with the operations of the vocal organs. The problem of tone-production is thus seen to be one of psychology. It narrows down to this: What can interfere with the normal action of the voice and prevent the vocal organs from instinctively responding to the demands of the ear? A satisfactory answer to this problem will be found only by a consideration of all available knowledge of the voice, both empirical and scientific. This forms the material of the final division of the present work.

Part IV

VOCAL SCIENCE AND PRACTICAL VOICE CULTURE

CHAPTER I

THE CORRECT VOCAL ACTION

Two distinct lines of approach were laid down for studying the operations of the voice. First, the manner of investigation usually accepted as scientific. This is, to study the vocal mechanism; to determine, as far as possible, the laws of its operation, in accordance with the principles of anatomy, acoustics, mechanics, and psychology. Second, the manner of investigation generally called empirical. This begins with the observing of the tones of the voice, considered simply as sounds. From the tones we work back to the vocal organs and apply to them the information obtained by attentive listening. Both of these means of investigation have been utilized; we are now in possession of the most salient facts obtainable regarding the vocal action.

Separately considered, neither the scientific nor the empirical study of the voice is alone sufficient to inform us of the exact nature of the correct vocal action. The next step is therefore to combine the information obtained from the two sources, scientific analysis and empirical observation. Let us begin by summing up all the facts so far ascertained.

Tone-production in singing is a conscious and voluntary muscular operation. The vocal organs consist of a number of sets of voluntary muscles, of the bones and cartilages to which these muscles are attached, and of the nerves and nerve centers governing their actions. The precise nature of the muscular contractions of tone-production, whether correct or incorrect, is not known. These contractions occur in accordance with established laws of acoustics and mechanics. Under normal conditions the vocal organs instinctively respond to the demands of the singer, through the guidance of the sense of hearing. The ability of the vocal organs to adjust themselves properly may be upset by some influence apparently outside the singer's voluntary control. Study of the vocal mechanism does not inform us of the meaning of the correct vocal action, nor of the difference between this action and any other mode of operation of the voice.

Empirically considered, there is a striking difference between the correct vocal action and any other manner of tone-production. A perfect vocal tone awakens in the hearer a distinct set of auditory and muscular sensations. Attentively observed, the muscular sensations of the hearer indicate that the perfect vocal tone is produced by the balanced and harmonious action of all the muscles of the singer's vocal mechanism. In listening to perfect singing the hearer feels that every muscle of the singer's vocal organs is contracted with exactly the appropriate degree of strength. Any vocal tone of unsatisfactory sound awakens in the hearer a set of muscular sensations, the direct opposite of those indicating the correct vocal action. An incorrectly produced tone imparts to the hearer a sensation of stiffness and undue muscular tension, located more or less definitely in the throat. This sensation indicates that the singer's throat is stiffened by excessive muscular contraction. Further, this feeling of throat stiffness indicates to the hearer that the singer's vocal action would become correct if the undue muscular tension were relaxed.

Combining now the results of empirical and scientific investigation of the voice, throat stiffness is seen to be the interfering influence which disturbs the instinctive connection between voice and ear. Let us now consider the meaning of throat stiffness as a feature of incorrect tone-production. First, what is muscular stiffness?

All the voluntary muscles of the body are arranged in opposed pairs, sets, or groups. A typical pair of opposed muscles are the biceps and triceps of the upper arm. Contraction of the biceps flexes the forearm at the elbow; the contrary movement, extending the forearm, results from the contraction of the triceps. This principle of opposition applies to the entire muscular system. One set of muscles raises the ribs in inspiration, another set lowers them in expiration; one group flexes the fingers and clenches the fist, an opposed set extends the fingers and opens the hand. Muscular opposition does not imply that the entire structure is made up of parallel pairs of muscles, like the biceps and triceps, located on opposite sides of the same bone. It means only that the opposed sets pull in contrary directions.

Each opposed set consists of muscles of about equal strength. Under normal conditions of relaxation the entire muscular system exerts a slight degree of contraction. To this normal state of oppositional contraction the name "muscular tonicity" is given. The present purpose does not call for a discussion of the subject of muscular tonicity. This form of contraction has no direct bearing on the performance of voluntary movements.

What effect has the voluntary contraction of all the muscles of any member, each opposed set exerting the same degree of strength? No motion of the member results, but the member is brought on tension and stiffened. This is well illustrated in the case of the arm. Extend the arm and clench the fist; then contract all the muscles of the arm, about as the athlete does to display his muscular development. You will notice that the arm becomes stiff and tense.

This state of tension is commonly called "muscular stiffness," but the term is open to objection. It is really the joints which are stiffened, not the muscles. We are, however, so accustomed to speak of muscular stiffness, and particularly of throat stiffness, that little is to be gained by substituting a more accurate expression.

A condition of muscular stiffness results from the contraction of all the muscles of a member, whether this contraction be voluntary or involuntary. This condition does not prevent the normal movements of the member; it only renders the movements more difficult and fatiguing and less effective. It is readily seen why this is the case. More than the necessary strength is exerted by the muscles. Suppose the biceps and triceps, for example, each to be contracted with five units of strength; then let some work be performed by the flexing of the forearm, requiring the exertion of two units of strength. In this case the biceps must exert two units of strength more than the triceps, that is, seven units. In all, the two muscles together exert twelve units of strength to accomplish the effective result of two units. Six times the needed strength is exerted. Activity of this kind is naturally fatiguing.

Muscular stiffness increases the difficulty of complex movements. Not only is unnecessary strength exerted; the stiffness of the joints also interferes with the freedom and facility of motion. But this unfavorable condition does not upset the power of coordination. The instinctive connection between the nerve centers of consciousness and the motor centers is not broken. Although hampered in their efforts, the muscles are still able to execute the demands of consciousness.

As an illustration of this analysis of muscular stiffness let us consider the actions of writing, when performed under the conditions just described. It is possible to write with the hand and arm in a state of muscular stiffness. But one does not write so easily, so rapidly, nor so well with the arm stiff as with the arm normally relaxed. Closer attention must be paid to the forming of the letters, and more effort must be put forth to write with the muscles stiffened; yet the result is not equal to that obtained with less care and labor under normal muscular conditions.

All that has been said of muscular stiffness applies with especial force to the vocal organs. Like the rest of the muscular system, the muscles of the vocal organs are arranged in opposed pairs and sets. The contraction of all the muscles of the throat, each opposed set or pair exerting about the same degree of strength, causes a condition of throat stiffness. Singing is possible in this condition. But the singer's command of the voice is not so complete and satisfactory as under normal conditions.

Throat stiffness does not altogether deprive the vocal organs of their faculty of instinctive adjustment in obedience to the demands of the ear. To a fair extent the voice is under the command of the singer. The vocal cords adjust themselves readily enough for the desired pitch; tones of the various degrees of loudness and softness can be sung in a fairly satisfactory manner. But the muscles are somewhat hampered in their contractions, and the response to the demands of the ear is not quite perfect. This lack of perfect command is evidenced specially in the quality of the tones. Some form of throaty quality always mars the voice when the throat is in a stiffened condition. In this regard the voice refuses to fulfill the demands of the ear. Even though the singer hears, and indeed feels, the effects of the muscular tension, and strives to remedy the fault of production, the voice still refuses to respond.

This incomplete command of the voice is frequently observed, even among singers of very high standing. At first sight the condition here described seems to disprove the statement that the voice normally obeys the ear. But there is no real contradiction of the psychological law of vocal command in the case of a stiff-throated singer. For one thing, whatever degree of command the singer possesses is obtained in accordance with the law of guidance by the ear. Moreover, the failure to secure perfect response is due solely to the interference with the normal workings of the voice, occasioned by the state of throat stiffness. Far from this form of muscular contraction being a contradiction of psychological principles, it will be found on examination to be in perfect accord with well-established laws of physiological psychology.

It is hardly to be supposed that the singer consciously and voluntarily contracts the muscles of the entire vocal mechanism and so deliberately brings about the stiffening of the throat. True, this can readily be done. We can at will sing throaty and nasal tones. But this form of voluntary throat tension is not, properly speaking, an incorrect vocal action. So long as the vocal organs respond to the demands of the ear, the vocal action is correct. Only when the voice refuses to obey can the action be described as incorrect.

A satisfactory definition of the various modes of vocal action can now be given. The correct vocal action is the natural operation of the vocal organs; the voice normally obeys the commands of the ear. An incorrect vocal action occurs when the throat is stiffened by the involuntary contraction of the muscles of the vocal mechanism.

This definition of the vocal action does not solve the problem of tone-production. It is still to be determined how the involuntary contraction of the throat muscles is caused.

CHAPTER II

THE CAUSES OF THROAT STIFFNESS AND OF INCORRECT VOCAL ACTION

Involuntary contractions of the voluntary muscles can occur only as reflex actions. If the muscles of the vocal organs are subject to involuntary contractions, the causes of these contractions must be sought through an investigation of the subject of reflex actions.

Reflex actions are of several kinds; of these the simplest type, and the one most easily studied, is the muscular contraction due to the excitation of the sensory nerve endings located in the skin. Thus when the sole of the foot of a sleeping person is tickled, the leg is at first drawn up and then violently kicked out. An exhaustive discussion of the physiological and psychological features of reflex action is not called for here; a sufficient understanding of the subject may safely be assumed to be possessed by the reader.

Involuntary muscular contractions often occur as reflex actions without any direct or tactual irritation of the sensory nerve endings. Several examples of this form of reflex action are now to be considered. These actions will be seen to be matters of such common experience as to call for no special proof. They are the following:

(a) Reflex actions performed under the influence of sensory impressions other than those of touch or muscular sense.

(b) Involuntary muscular contractions due to nervousness.

(c) Contractions of the muscles of certain members, caused by the turning of the attention specially to the members.

(d) Involuntary contractions of muscles, accompanying the exertion of other associated and antagonist muscles, and due to the radiation of nerve impulse.

(a) Reflex Actions due to Sensory Impressions other than those of Touch or Muscular Sense

A wide range of movements is included under this heading. Of these it is necessary to mention only a few, such as the sudden start on the hearing of an unexpected noise, the instinctive movement of dodging to escape an approaching missile, and the raising of the arm to ward off an expected blow.

Actions of a somewhat similar character normally occur in which it is not easy to point to the excitation of any sense or senses. These include the instinctive cowering attitude of fear, the play of facial expression caused by sentiment and emotion, etc.

(b) Involuntary Actions due to Nervousness

A condition of marked nervousness generally causes the involuntary contraction of muscles. Who does not recall his earliest attempts at "speaking a piece" in school? The trembling of the lips, the twitching of the arms and hands, and the vain attempts to govern the bodily movements, are an experience painful even in the recollection.

Movements and contractions due to nervousness are entirely purposeless; they even defy the most earnest efforts at inhibition. A marked feature of this type of involuntary action is the contraction of antagonist groups of muscles, productive of muscular stiffness of the members.

An extreme example of this form of nervousness is offered by the unfortunate sufferer from stage fright. In this condition the entire body often stiffens, and purposeful movement of any kind becomes for a time impossible.

(c) Contractions caused by Special Attention to Certain Members

Suppose a small boy of sensitive nature to enter a room suddenly, and to be at once chided for his awkwardness. His body will probably stiffen, and his awkwardness become more pronounced. Now call his attention to his hands and tell him he is holding them badly. His arms and hands will immediately become painfully stiff. Speak of his feet and his legs come on tension. Whatever member his attention is turned to, the muscles of that part contract involuntarily.

Photographers sometimes have to contend with this form of involuntary action on the part of their sitters. When the hands are to be posed the arms stiffen; so also do the legs, the shoulders, and the neck, each when its turn comes to receive attention.

Under normal conditions this form of awkwardness is easily overcome. Sitting for a photograph soon becomes a simple matter. The boy outgrows the awkward stage and gradually acquires a natural and easy bearing. Muscular stiffening due to attention to special members is usually the result of an uncomfortable feeling of being out of one's element, and ill at ease in one's surroundings. So soon as this feeling wears off the tendency to this form of stiffness disappears.

(d) Contractions of Muscles due to the Radiation of Nerve Impulse

A voluntary exertion of some of the muscles of a member sometimes causes the involuntary contraction of all the other muscles of the part. As will readily be seen, the exercise then takes place under conditions of muscular stiffness. This is commonly a feature of the unskilful and unaccustomed performance of muscular activities. A few examples will serve to illustrate this type of involuntary contraction better than a lengthy discussion of the physio-psychological principles involved.

When a novice takes his first lesson in riding a bicycle he clutches the handle bars in a vise-like grip. His knees are so stiff as to bend only with a great exertion of strength. To steer the wheel the learner must put forth his most powerful muscular efforts. A half-hour lesson in bicycle riding often tires the beginner more than an afternoon's ride does the experienced cyclist.

This condition of muscular stiffness is due to the contraction of antagonist groups of muscles, involving practically the entire body. In one sense the excessive muscular contractions are involuntary; yet it would not be easy to define where the voluntary element of the contractions leaves off.

A similar excessive expenditure of strength may be seen in the attempt of an illiterate laborer to sign his name. He grips the pen as though it were a crowbar, and puts forth enough strength to handle a twenty-pound weight. Learning to dance, or to skate, or to row a boat, is usually accompanied in the beginning by this form of muscular stiffness.

As skill is acquired by practice in the performance of complex activities, the undue muscular tension of the initial stage is gradually relaxed.

There is another way in which the radiation of nerve impulse may be caused, entirely distinct from the lack of use or skill. Muscular stiffness may be induced in the case of activities so thoroughly habitual as to be normally performed automatically. The cause of muscular stiffness now to be considered is the attempt to perform complex activities mechanically, that is, by consciously directing the individual component movements and muscular contractions involved in the actions. Involuntary contractions of associated and antagonist muscles take place under these conditions, in addition to the voluntary exercise of the muscles normally exerted in the movements.

This fact may be illustrated by attempting to write a few lines, and forming every stroke of each letter by a distinct exercise of the will. If you keep up this attempt for ten minutes you will find that you press upon the paper with many times your accustomed weight. The hand stiffens in consequence of the close attention paid to its movements. This stiffness will extend to the arm, and even to the shoulder, if the exercise be continued long enough and with sufficient intensity of attention to the hand.

Another good illustration of this form of muscular stiffening may be found by walking upstairs, and paying the same kind of attention to the muscular actions. Try to ascend a single flight of stairs, performing each elementary movement by a distinct volitional impulse. Pause on the first step to secure perfect balance on one foot; raise the other foot, bending the leg at the knee, then place this foot carefully on the next higher step. Now gradually shift the weight of the body from the lower to the higher foot; as the body inclines forward, exert the muscles of the back and sides to preserve your balance; then contract the leg muscles so as to raise the body to the higher step, with the weight supported on that foot. Repeat this operation for each step. To mount one flight of stairs in this way will tire you more than ascending a half dozen flights in the ordinary automatic way.

All four of the types of involuntary muscular contraction just described may be combined in a single instance. An inexperienced violin soloist, such as a student playing at a conservatory recital, often exemplifies this. Nervousness and awkwardness cause him to tremble; the scratchy sound of his tones makes him twitch and start; meanwhile, the close attention paid to his fingering and bowing stiffens his arms and completes his difficulty.

The vocal organs are peculiarly subject to the forms of involuntary muscular contraction under consideration. Each of the causes of muscular tension may exert its special influence on the voice. Let us go over the ground once more, this time with special reference to the actions of the throat muscles.

(a) Reflex Actions of the Muscles of the Vocal Organs, Independent of Direct Sensory Excitation

Involuntary actions of the vocal organs normally occur in response to stimuli furnished by the emotions and feelings. Every one is familiar with the shout of triumph, the sigh of relief, and the ejaculation of surprise. Some emotions cause a convulsive stiffening of the muscles of the vocal organs so complete as to render tone-production for a time absolutely impossible. "Speechless with terror," "breathless with apprehension," are expressions which accurately describe psychological processes. A crowd of people watching a difficult rescue of a drowning man is silent so long as the uncertainty lasts. A shout instantly goes up when the rescue is seen to be safely effected. Both the silence of the nervous strain and the shout of relief are normal involuntary responses to the emotional states.

(b) The Influence of Nervousness on the Vocal Action

Nervous conditions exert a striking influence on the operations of the voice. Even when our self-control under trying conditions is complete in all other respects we are often unable to prevent our voices betraying our nervous state. Stage fright, an extreme form of nervousness, sometimes deprives the sufferer entirely of the power of speech. This temporary loss of vocal command is not due to an inability to innervate the muscles of the vocal organs; on the contrary, it is caused by extreme muscular stiffness due to the violent, though involuntary, contraction of all the muscles of the vocal organs.

Under normal conditions, entirely aside from nervousness, the voice instinctively reflects every phase of sentiment and emotion. Love and hate, sorrow and joy, anger, fear, and rage, each is clearly expressed by the quality of the tones, independent of the meaning of the spoken words. All these fine shades of tone quality result from muscular adjustments of the vocal mechanism. In some mysterious manner the outflow of motor impulses to the throat muscles is governed by the nervous and emotional states.

This form of muscular contraction is in one sense not involuntary. As the voice is voluntarily used, all the muscular contractions involved are voluntary. Yet the minute contractions producing tone qualities expressive of emotion are distinctly involuntary. More than this, these contractions cannot usually be inhibited. An angry man cannot make his voice sound other than angry. Our voices often betray our feelings in spite of the most earnest efforts at concealment.

While the voice always normally and involuntarily adopts the tone quality indicative of the emotional state, this action of the vocal organs may be voluntarily and purposely performed. A perfect command of these fine shades of tone quality renders the voice a very potent instrument of expression. For the purposes of dramatic singing this form of vocal expression might be of great value. It is to be regretted that dramatic singers of this day pay so little attention to purely tonal expressiveness. This is probably due in great measure to the prevalence of throat stiffness, which robs the voice of much of its expressive power.

(c) Contractions of the Throat Muscles, caused by Attention to the Throat

When a physician attempts to examine a child's throat, the tendency of the throat muscles to this form of involuntary contractions is apt to be evidenced. The jaw stiffens and the tongue rises; for a time the rebellious little throat refuses to remain quiet and relaxed.

People usually have some such difficulty the first time they submit to examination with the laryngoscope. This is very apt to occur, even in the case of experienced singers. Needless to say, this form of muscular contraction is entirely involuntary; it even defies the most earnest attempts at prevention. Comparatively little experience is required for normal people to overcome this tendency. The throat usually becomes tractable after one or two trials with the laryngoscope.

Vocalists are well aware of the proneness of one part of the vocal mechanism, the tongue, to stiffen in consequence of direct attention being paid to this member. In this connection Frang鐵 n-Davies remarks: "When the writer in early student days concentrated his attention upon his tongue he found that this member became very stiff and unruly indeed." (The Singing of the Future, London, 1906.) Leo Kofler speaks of the same tendency: "Tell a pupil to let his tongue lie flat in his mouth; he draws it back till it dams up his throat." (Werner's Magazine, Oct., 1899.)

(d) Throat Stiffness due to the Radiation of Nerve Impulse

Two types of muscular tension due to the radiation of motor impulses were noted; first, the stiffness incident to the early stages of practice in complex activities; second, the stiffness caused by the attempt to perform complex activities in a mechanical manner by paying attention to the individual component movements and contractions. To both these types of muscular stiffness the voice is especially subject.

It is not easy to find a perfect illustration of throat stiffness incident to the early stages of instruction in singing. For this the chief reason is that the later form of stiffness, due to the attempt directly to manage the vocal organs, is much more pronounced than the temporary early tension. As good an example as possible would be the following: Let some one possessed of a fine natural untrained voice sing a steady tone and then attempt to trill on the same note. The attempted trill will invariably indicate a much higher degree of stiffness than the single tone.

Several investigators of the voice have noticed the tendency of the throat to stiffen when the singer tries to manage the voice by paying direct attention to the mechanical action. Clara Kathleen Rogers points this out clearly in the following passage: "There exists a possible and a dangerous obstacle to the performance of the natural mission of the voice. That obstacle is what? It is a superfluous and misdirected mental activity which is fruitful of a corresponding obstruction on the part of the body. In the body this obstruction takes the form of superfluous or unnatural tension." (The Philosophy of Singing, N. Y., 1893.) Prof. Scripture describes in scientific language the results of any attempt directly to manage the vocal organs. Speaking of the use of the voice under unfavorable conditions, he says: "The attempt is instinctively made by the speaker or singer to correct such a fault by voluntary innervation of the muscles; this cannot succeed perfectly because an increase of innervation brings about contractions of associated and antagonist muscles with the result of changed conditions and changed sounds. Such extra muscular effort is, moreover, very fatiguing." (The Elements of Experimental Phonetics, 1902.)

For the purposes of scientific voice culture this is one of the most important facts which have been determined. The attempt to manage the voice, by paying attention to the mechanical operations of the vocal organs, causes an involuntary contraction of all the throat muscles, and so interferes with the normal instinctive vocal action. Even the mere thinking of the throat in singing, and especially in practising, is enough to induce throat stiffness.

CHAPTER III

THROAT STIFFNESS AND INCORRECT SINGING

It is a lamentable fact that most of the singing heard nowadays gives evidence of throat stiffness. Perfect singing becomes more rare with each succeeding year. The younger generation of artists in particular evince a marked tendency to this fault of production.

Considered as a cause of faulty tone-production in singing, throat stiffness is due to only one influence, viz., the attempt to manage the voice by thinking of the vocal organs and their mechanical operations. Muscular tension due to nervousness, or to the unskilful nature of first attempts at singing, cannot be looked upon as causing a wrong vocal action. In the case of nervousness the lack of vocal command faithfully reflects the psychological condition of the singer; the imperfect response of the voice is normal to this condition. The stiffness due to first attempts is also perfectly normal. Moreover, both these forms of throat stiffness are temporary; they disappear when the cause, nervousness or lack of skill, is removed.

Throat stiffness does not necessarily destroy the musical character of the voice. Very many degrees and varieties of excessive throat tension are possible. The undue muscular exertion may be so slight in degree that the throat stiffness can be detected in the sound of the tones only by a highly sensitive and observant hearer. Or on the other hand, the muscles of the entire throat may be so powerfully contracted that the singer has only a very imperfect command of the voice. Between the two extremes, perfect tone-production and exaggerated stiffness, every conceivable shade of difference in degree of undue tension might be illustrated in the case of some prominent singer.

Faulty tone-production manifests itself in two ways; first, in its effects on the tones of the voice; second, in its effects on the singer's throat. Let us consider each of these topics separately.

The Effect of Throat Stiffness on the Sound of the Voice

In whatever degree throat stiffness is present, to just that extent the voice sacrifices something of its capabilities as a musical instrument. The voice can realize its full natural resources of beauty, range, power, and flexibility only when the throat is absolutely free from undue tension. As regards the quality of the tones, every phase of undue throat tension has its effect on the sound of the voice. These effects are always bad; the same voice is less beautiful when used in a stiffened condition than when perfectly produced. Throaty and nasal tones are always more or less harsh and offensive to the sensitive hearer. Further, the more pronounced the state of throat stiffness the more marked does the throaty or nasal quality become.

Under conditions of throat tension the range of the voice is almost always curtailed. The highest and lowest notes possible to any voice can be reached only when the throat is entirely free from stiffness. So also with regard to the varying degrees of power, undue tension prevents the singer from obtaining the extreme effects. A throaty singer's soft tones generally lack the carrying quality. Louder tones can be produced with a normally relaxed than with a stiffened throat.

Real flexibility of voice is impossible to a stiff-throated singer. Extreme rapidity and accuracy of muscular adjustments, the physical basis of coloratura singing, cannot be attained when the muscles are hampered by undue tension.

A distinct fault of production, the tremolo, is directly due to throat stiffness. A simple experiment illustrates the nature of the muscular action from which the tremolo results. "Set" the muscles of the arm by contracting the biceps and triceps with the utmost possible strength. With the arm in this stiffened condition flex and extend the forearm slowly several times. You will notice a pronounced trembling of the arm. Why a condition of muscular stiffness should cause the affected member to tremble is not well understood. But the fact admits of no question. It is highly probable that the tremolo is caused by a trembling of the vocal organs, due to muscular stiffness. The tones of a voice afflicted with tremolo always give evidence of extreme throat tension.

Another bad result of throat stiffness in tone-production is seen in the matter of intonation. Tones produced with a stiff throat are seldom in perfect tune. This subject will be more fully treated in a later chapter.

Effects of Muscular Stiffness on the Throat

Many of the muscles of the vocal organs, particularly the laryngeal muscles, are extremely small and delicate. Under normal conditions these muscles are fully capable of exerting the relatively small amount of strength required of them without strain or injury. But when the voice is used in a stiffened condition the delicate muscles of the larynx are obliged to contract with much more than their normal strength. To borrow an expression of the engineers, the throat muscles are then forced to carry an excessive load.

A balanced contraction of antagonist groups of muscles is the muscular basis of throat stiffness. When the voice is used in this condition each muscle of the vocal organs must put forth the amount of effort necessary to produce the desired effect under normal conditions, in addition to an effort equal to the counterbalancing pull of its antagonist muscle. An increase in the degree of throat stiffness demands a corresponding increase in the effort exerted by every muscle of the throat.

Over-exertion of muscles always results in strain and injury. The extent of the injury to the muscular tissues varies with the degree of excessive exertion and with the duration of the injurious exercise. An advanced stage of muscular strain is distinctly a pathological condition.

Tone-production in a state of throat stiffness is of necessity injurious to the muscles of the vocal organs. The delicate laryngeal muscles are specially subject to the injurious effects of strain. These effects vary in extent and character, according to the degree of throat stiffness, to the extent and duration of the faulty use of the voice, and to the individual characteristics of the singer. A very slight degree of undue tension may not sensibly injure the voice. Even a fairly marked condition of tension, such as is evidenced by the uniformly throaty quality of many baritones and mezzo-sopranos, may be persisted in for years without perceptibly straining the throat or destroying the musical value of the voice. But a misuse of the voice is bound, in the course of time, to show its injurious results on the throat. How many promising young singers are forced to abandon their careers in early life, at the time when their artistic and dramatic powers are just ripening to fruition! A misused voice "wears out" years before its time.

Most of the throat troubles of singers are directly caused by throat stiffness and muscular strain. Dr. Mills, among others, touches on this fact. "All the author's experience as a laryngologist tended to convince him that most of those evils from which speakers and singers suffer, whatever the part of the vocal mechanism affected, arise from faulty methods of voice production, or excess in the use of methods in themselves correct." (Voice Production in Singing and Speaking, Phila., 1906.)

For the purposes of artistic singing, a voice loses all its value when the injurious effects of throat stiffness become very pronounced. On this account singers are obliged to give up appearing in public before the condition reaches the extreme. It follows therefore that only in the case of public speakers do we see the extreme results of persistence in the wrong use of the voice. "Clergyman's sore throat" is the name usually applied to this condition. The sustained use of the voice, under conditions of extreme strain, is exceedingly painful both to the speaker and to the hearer.

Singers are usually unconscious of throat stiffness unless the condition be very pronounced. Neither the sense of hearing nor the muscular sense informs the singer of the state of tension. Accustomed to the sound of his own voice, the singer may be unaware of a throaty or nasal quality which he would instantly detect in another voice. This is also true of the muscular sensations of tone-production; habit makes the singer inattentive to the sensations caused by throat tension.

Throat stiffness always tends to become greater in degree; it is a self-aggravating condition. Even though very slight in its beginnings, the state of stiffness obliges the singer to put forth more than the normal effort in order to secure the desired effects. This increase of innervation is not confined to the muscles which need to be more strongly contracted. As Prof. Scripture points out, it also extends to the associated and antagonist muscles, that is, to all the muscles of the throat. Thus the stiffness is increased in degree. Still greater exertion is then required, resulting in still greater stiffness. This may go on for years, the voice gradually becoming less responsive to the demands of the singer.

Individual personal characteristics are an important factor in determining a singer's experience with throat stiffness. Some singers are so fortunately constituted as to be almost entirely free from the tendency to stiffen the throat. Others detect the tendency in its beginning and find no difficulty in correcting it. Still others habituate themselves to some manner of tone-production, and neither increase nor diminish the degree of stiffness. Even under modern methods of instruction, many artists are correctly trained from the start and so never stiffen their throats in any way.

Several traits of character are concerned in determining the individual tendency to throat stiffness. Nervous temperament, keenness of ear, artistic and musical endowment, each has its influence in this connection.

The great prevalence of throat stiffness among present-day singers is due primarily to the idea of mechanical vocal management as the basis of instruction in singing. Not only are modern methods intrinsically worthless, in that a correct use of the voice cannot be attained by the application of mechanical rules. Worse than this, the means used for training the voice are such as to defeat their own purpose. At every instant of instruction the student's attention is expressly turned to the vocal organs and to the mechanical operations of the voice. The only possible result of this kind of vocal instruction is to stiffen the throat and so to render the correct vocal action an impossibility.

A peculiar contradiction is presented by the modern vocal teacher; his artistic conception of singing is utterly at variance with his ideas of mechanical tone-production. It may safely be said that the vast majority of vocal teachers are thoroughly conversant with the highest standards of artistic singing. They know what effects their pupils ought to obtain. But the means they use for enabling the pupils to get these effects have exactly the contrary result. When the student tries to open the throat this obstinate organ only closes the tighter. Attempting to correct a tremolo by "holding the throat steady" causes the throat to tremble all the more.

Modern voice culture, in its practical aspect, is a struggle with throat stiffness. Everything the student does, for the purpose of acquiring direct command of the voice, has some influence in causing the throat to stiffen. Telling the student to hold the throat relaxed seldom effects a cure; this direction includes a primary cause of tension,--the turning of attention to the throat. All the teacher can do to counteract the stiffening influence is to give relaxing exercises. These are in most cases efficacious so long as constructive instruction is abandoned, and the relaxing of the throat is made the sole purpose of study. But soon after positive instruction is resumed the tendency to stiffen reappears. As lesson follows after lesson, the stiffness becomes gradually, imperceptibly more pronounced. At length the time again comes for relaxing exercises.

A single repetition of this process, relaxing the throat and then stiffening it again, may extend over several months of study. During this time the student naturally learns a great deal about music and the artistic side of singing, and also improves the keenness of the sense of hearing. This artistic development is necessarily reflected in the voice so soon as the throat is again relaxed.

It usually happens that students change teachers about the time the voice has become unmanageably stiff. In this condition the student, of course, sings rather badly. A marked improvement in the singing generally results from the change of teachers. This is easy to understand because the new teacher devotes his first efforts to relaxing the stiffened throat. Later on this improvement is very likely to be lost, for the second teacher has nothing more of a positive nature to offer than the first.

Vocal teachers in general seem to be aware of the fact that mechanical instruction causes the student's throat to stiffen. A much-debated question is whether "local effort" is needed to bring about the correct vocal action. The term local effort is used to describe the direct innervation of the throat muscles. A logical application of the mechanical idea absolutely demands the use of local effort. This is the main argument of the local-effort teachers.

Those teachers who discountenance local effort have only their own experience to guide them. They simply know that local effort results in throat stiffness. Yet these teachers have nothing to offer in place of the mechanical management of the vocal organs. Even though aware of the evil results of local effort, they yet know of no other means of imparting the correct vocal action. The weakness of the position of these teachers is well summed up by a writer in Werner's Magazine for June, 1899: "To teach without local effort or local thought is to teach in the dark. Every exponent of the non-local-effort theory contradicts his theory every time he tells of it." To that extent this writer states the case correctly. Every modern vocal teacher believes that the voice must be consciously guided in its muscular operations. Until this erroneous belief is abandoned it is idle for a teacher to decry the use of local effort.

CHAPTER IV

THE TRUE MEANING OF VOCAL TRAINING

In all scientific treatises on the voice it is assumed that the voice has some specifically correct mode of operation. Training the voice is supposed to involve the leading of the vocal organs to abandon their natural and instinctive manner of operating, and to adopt some other form of activity. Further, the assumption is made that the student of singing must cause the vocal organs to adopt a supposedly correct manner of operating by paying direct attention to the mechanical movements of tone-production. Both these assumptions are utterly mistaken. On scientific analysis no difference is seen between the right and the wrong vocal action, such as is assumed in the accepted Vocal Science. Psychological principles do not countenance the idea of mechanical vocal management.

Yet the fact remains, as a matter of empirical observation, that there is a marked difference between the natural voice and the correctly trained voice. What change takes place in the voice as a result of correct training?

Singing is a natural function of the vocal organs. Learning to sing artistically does not involve a departure from natural and instinctive processes. The training of the voice consists of the acquirement of skill in the use of the vocal organs, and of nothing more.

Under normal conditions the vocal organs instinctively adjust themselves, by performing the necessary muscular contractions, to fulfill the demands of the ear. In order that a perfect musical tone be produced it is necessary in the first place that the ear be keen and well trained; only such an ear can know the exact sound of a perfect tone, and so demand it of the voice. Second, the vocal organs must make repeated efforts to produce the perfect tone, each response approaching nearer to the mentally-conceived tone. Two elements are therefore involved in the training of the voice; first, the cultivation of the sense of hearing; second, the acquirement of skill in the use of the voice by the actual practice of singing.

Practical vocal teachers generally recognize the importance of both these elements of Voice Culture. Only in one way do they fall short of fully realizing the value of ear training and of practice guided by the ear;--they do not see that these two topics sum up the whole material of vocal training. Unfortunately, the search after some imaginary means of direct vocal management destroys, in all modern methods, most of the value of the real elements of voice culture.

A few citations from standard writers on the voice will show the estimation in which ear-training is held. To begin with, the old Italian masters were fully alive to the necessity of cultivating the sense of hearing, as witness Tosi: "One who has not a good ear should not undertake either to instruct or to sing." This writer also says in the chapter headed "Observations for a student": "Let him hear as much as he can the most celebrated singers, and likewise the most excellent instrumental performers; because from the attention in hearing them one reaps more advantage than from any instruction whatsoever."

Another early writer on the voice, the celebrated Adolph Bernhard Marx, speaks of the advantage derived from the attentive listening to voices: "An important influence is exerted by the frequent attentive hearing of good voices. Through this an idea of good tone is strengthened, which gains an influence on the use and also on the training of the organs, not perhaps immediate, but clearly seen in its results." (Die Kunst des Gesanges, Berlin, 1826.)

Among modern writers only a few need be mentioned. D. Frangen-Davies remarks: "The training of the ear is one half of the training of the voice." (The Singing of the Future.) Clara Kathleen Rogers is even more emphatic in her statement: "Not to exercise our sense of hearing is to rob it gradually of the habit of acting at all; whereas, if we keep it in exercise, it will daily grow readier, finer, more acute, more analytical, and the ear will serve as an ever more effective medium of reaction on the will." The following remark of the same writer points unmistakably to an understanding of the evil results of the attempt to sing mechanically: "If the singer's attention is directed to any part of the vocal instrument, or even to its motor, the breath, his sense of sound, and his perception of either the beautiful or the bad elements in sound, will grow fainter and fainter." (The Physiology of Singing.)

As for the purpose of cultivating the sense of hearing, this is also pointed out by several prominent vocal theorists. One of the latest exponents of the traditional method of instruction was St 聞 hen de la Madelaine, who remarks: "The first need of the voice is to be guided in its exercise by an ear capable of appreciating naturally its least deviation." (Theorie complete du Chant, Paris, 1852.)

One of the most recent authoritative writers on voice culture, Dr. Mills, speaks at length of the necessity of guiding the voice by the sense of hearing. "We cannot too much insist on both speaker and singer attending to forming a connection between his ear and his mouth cavity. He is to hear that he may produce good tones, and the tones cannot be correctly formed if they be not well observed. To listen to one's self carefully and constantly is a most valuable but little practised art. The student should listen as an inexorable critic, accepting only the best from himself." Dr. Mills touches on the psychological features of the connection between voice and ear. "There can be no doubt that the nervous impulses that pass from the ear to the brain are of all sensory messages the most important guides for the outgoing ones that determine the necessary movements." Summing up the matter of ear-training and vocal guidance Dr. Mills says: "The author would impress on all students of music, and of the voice as used in both singing and speaking, the paramount importance of learning early to listen most attentively to others when executing music; and above all to listen with the greatest care to themselves, and never to accept any musical tone that does not fully satisfy the ear." (Voice Production in Singing and Speaking, 1906.)

One more citation from Mrs. Rogers must suffice. "And now, in conclusion, let me once more remind the singer that in practising these and all other vocal exercises the ear is the only safe guide."

Given a fine natural voice and a trained musical ear, skill is acquired in the use of the voice by the repetition of effort. The only necessity is for the singer to have a clear mental conception of the effects to be obtained, and to listen attentively to the voice. With each repetition of an exercise, whether on sustained tones, scale passages, crescendo and diminuendo, or whatever else, the voice responds more smoothly and accurately to the mental demand. Each time the student practises the exercise he listens to the tones and notes how they differ from the desired effect; he strives the next time to correct this departure.

Psychological principles verify the proverb that practice makes perfect. This is true of all complex activities. Through repeated performance the muscles, or rather the motor-nerve centers, become habituated to complex activities. Coordinations gradually become perfect and automatic because the nerve impulses naturally tend to take the well-worn paths. To this rule the voice is no exception. Practice makes perfect, with the voice, as with every other muscular activity.

In practical Voice Culture the ear and the voice are normally trained together. The proper function of the teacher is to guide the student in developing along the two lines. Listening to his own voice is a valuable means for the student to develop his sense of hearing. It is for the master to point out the salient qualities and faults in the pupil's tones in order that the pupil may know what to listen for. As the ear gradually becomes keener and better acquainted with the characteristics of perfect singing, it also becomes more exacting in its demands on the voice. In its turn the voice steadily improves in its responsiveness to the ear.

Skill in using the voice involves something more than has thus far been considered under the head of tone-production. Skill in singing is synonymous with finished vocal technique, and the basis of technique is the correctly produced single tone. It is seen that a single tone can be sung correctly when, first, the singer knows the sound of the perfect musical tone, and second, the vocal organs are not hampered by muscular stiffness. When these conditions are fulfilled nothing but practice is needed for the acquirement of technical skill.

Coloratura singing presents the highest development of vocal technique. Dazzling as the effects of coloratura are, they are obtained by the combination of a few simple elements. Perfect command of the single tone throughout the entire compass of the voice, with accurately graded crescendo and diminuendo, the clear, rapid, and accurate transition from one note to another in the varying degrees of staccato and legato,--these elements include the whole physical material of vocal technique.

Training the voice is one concrete process. Its component features may be considered separately; the cultivation of the sense of hearing, the acquirement of command of the single tone, and the development of technical skill,--each may be considered apart from its companion processes. But in actual practice the three elements of Voice Culture cannot be dissociated. The student of singing progresses simultaneously along all three lines. Intelligently directed practice in singing results in this simultaneous progress. As the voice depends for guidance on the ear, so the ear benefits by the improvement of the voice. Each advance made by the voice toward the perfect production of tone is marked by a greater facility in the technical use of the voice. Correct tone-production cannot be directly acquired by the singing of single tones. This practice would tend to stiffen the throat. Technique and tone-production must be developed together.

There is a difference between the natural and the properly trained voice. As to the nature of this difference the facts of empirical observation are borne out by the results of scientific analysis. The natural voice is crude because it is unskilfully used. A lack of facility is revealed in the untrained singer's handling of the voice. Intonations are imperfect; transitions from note to note are rough; the whole effect indicates that the voice is not completely under the command of the singer. Further, the sound of the individual tones betrays faults of production. The tones are more or less throaty or nasal, or indicative of some degree of muscular tension.

A perfectly used voice, on the other hand, convinces the hearer that the singer has full command of all the resources of the vocal organs. Each tone is a perfect musical sound, free from fault or blemish. The voice moves from one note to another with ease and with purity of intonation. All the gradations of loud and soft, all the lights and shades of sentiment or passion, seem to respond directly to the singer's instinctive desire for musical expression. On the physical side the singer's voice is felt by the hearer to be in a condition of balanced and harmonious muscular activity.

When the possessor of a good natural voice goes through a proper course of vocal training, the faults of production native to the untrained voice are gradually corrected. Wrong muscular tension is imperceptibly relaxed. Little by little the student acquires facility in handling the voice. Coincident with this progress is the advance toward the correct vocal action. The transition from the natural to the perfect use of the voice is gradual and imperceptible. There is no stage of progress at which the operations of the voice radically change in character. At no time does the student change the manner of managing the voice. Effects difficult at first gradually become easier, simply as the result of practice. This is the only change that the voice undergoes in training.

One influence, and only one, can interfere with this normal development of the voice. This is the involuntary and unconscious stiffening of the throat. In the normal practice of singing nothing is involved which could cause the throat to stiffen. True, the first stages of study are usually marked by a slight degree of stiffness, due solely to the lack of practice and experience. This initial stiffness does not tend to become habitual; it disappears before the student becomes aware of it, and leaves no permanent trace on the voice. That is, provided mechanical instruction does not intervene, to introduce the tendency directly to stiffen the throat.

As the initial stiffness disappears, and the vocal action gradually becomes smooth and automatic, the voice begins to take on the characteristics of perfect tone-production. The voice rounds out, the tones become free and true, and in perfect tune. No excessive throat tension being present, the voice conforms to the correct empirical standard of tone-production. It gives evidence to the ear of correct support and of open throat. The tones issue freely from the mouth and convey no impression of throat or nose.

As a matter of experience it is known that vocal students generally make satisfactory progress in the first few months of study. This is perfectly natural. It requires several months for the normally constituted student to grasp the idea of mechanical vocal management. Gifted with a fine voice, the natural impulse of any one is to sing. By singing naturally the voice is bound to improve.

Just so soon as the student begins to understand the meaning of attempted mechanical guidance of the voice, the evil effects of throat stiffness begin to be manifest. The more earnest and intelligent students are often the worst sufferers from throat stiffness. They more readily grasp the mechanical doctrines of modern methods and apply the mechanical idea more thoroughly.

There is in reality no problem of tone-production such as the accepted theory of Voice Culture propounds. The voice does not require to be taught how to act. Tone-production was never thought to involve any mechanical problem until the attention of vocalists was turned to the mechanical operations of the voice. This dates, roughly speaking, from about 1800. Since that time the whole tendency of Voice Culture has been mechanical. Nowadays the entire musical world is acquainted with the idea that the voice must be directly guided; hardly any one has ever heard this belief contradicted. To say that the voice needs no guidance other than the ear would seem utterly preposterous to the average lover of singing. It is even highly probable that this statement would not be understood. Yet there is strong evidence that the old Italian masters would have had equal difficulty in grasping the idea of mechanical vocal management. How long it will take for the vocal profession to be persuaded of the error of the mechanical idea only the future can determine.

Probably the most important fact about vocal training is the following: The voice is benefited by producing beautiful tones, and is injured by producing harsh sounds. A tone of perfect beauty can be sung only when the vocal organs are free from unnecessary tension. The nearer the tones approach to the perfection of beauty, the closer does the voice come to the correct action. Healthy exercise of the voice, with the throat free from strain, strengthens and develops the throat muscles. Harsh and unmusical sounds, produced by the voice, indicate that the throat is in a condition of injurious tension. Singing under these circumstances strains and weakens the muscles of the throat and injures the voice. The harsher the tones the worse they are for the voice.

Beauty of tone is the only criterion of the correct vocal action. By listening to himself the singer may know whether his tone-production is correct. If the tones are beautiful the tone-production cannot be wrong. The ear must always decide. A normally constituted ear instinctively delights in hearing beautiful sounds. While attentive listening renders the ear more keen and discriminating, no vocal student of average gifts need be told the meaning of tonal beauty.

Instinct prompts the possessor of a fine natural voice and a musical ear to sing, and to sing beautiful tones. No normally constituted student can take pleasure in the practice of mechanical exercises. This form of study is repugnant to the musical sensibility. Vocal students want to sing; they feel instinctively that the practice of mechanical exercises is not singing. A prominent exponent of mechanical instruction complains: "I tell them to take breathing exercises three times a day--but they all want to go right to singing songs." (Werner's Magazine, April, 1899.) These students are perfectly right. They know instinctively that the voice can be trained only by singing. There is no connection between artistic singing and the practice of toneless breathing exercises. "Five finger drills" and studies in broken scales of the types generally used are also utterly unmusical. Mechanical drills, whether toneless or vocal, have little effect other than to induce throat stiffness.

CHAPTER V

IMITATION THE RATIONAL BASIS OF VOICE CULTURE

It is generally assumed by vocal theorists that the voice cannot be trained by imitation. Browne and Behnke state this belief definitely: "Singing cannot be learned exclusively by imitation." (Voice, Song, and Speech.) Having ascertained the futility of the attempt to teach singing mechanically, it is now in order to determine the truth or falsity of the statement that the exercise of the imitative faculty alone does not suffice for the training of the voice.

In the first place, no one has ever thought of questioning the existence of an instinct of vocal imitation. On the contrary, this instinct is everywhere recognized. In childhood we learn to speak our mother tongue by imitating the speech of those about us. "Talking proper does not set in till the instinct to imitate sounds ripens in the nervous system." (The Principles of Psychology, Wm. James, New York, 1890.)

Vocal imitation would be impossible without the ability of the voice to produce sounds in obedience to the commands of the ear. This ability the voice normally possesses; spoken language could not otherwise exist. The voice can imitate a wide range of sounds. If the perfect vocal tone can be shown to be included in this range of sounds, then the voice can be trained by imitation.

Exceptional powers of vocal imitation are sometimes developed. Vaudeville performers are by no means rare who can imitate the tones of the oboe, the clarinet, the muted trumpet, and several other instruments. Imitation of the notes and songs of birds is also a familiar type of performance. This peculiar gift of imitation results in each case from some special structure of the vocal organs. One performer can imitate the reed instruments, another the lighter brasses, and so on. Just what peculiar formation of the vocal organs is required for this type of imitative ability need not be inquired here. All that need be noted is, that the vocal organs must be so constructed as to be able to produce the particular quality of sound. Given this natural ability on the part of the vocal organs, the power to produce the tone quality is developed by repeated attempts at imitation. The possessor of the natural gift perfects this gift by practice. For practice in the imitation of sounds to be effective it is necessary that the ear be well acquainted with the tone quality to be reproduced. In addition, the practice must be guided by the performer listening closely to the sounds produced by the vocal organs, and constantly comparing these sounds to the tones of the instrument chosen for imitation.

This vocal imitation of instruments is not a normal ability; the tones of the oboe and trumpet do not lie within the range of qualities native to the normal voice. But the quality of the perfect vocal tone is unquestionably within the range of every voice so constituted as to be capable of artistic singing. A fine natural voice normally produces beautiful tones. It is only with this type of voice that Voice Culture is concerned. Such a voice must be capable of producing the perfect vocal tone. Can it learn to produce this quality of tone by imitation?

It cannot be questioned that the faulty tones of one voice can readily be imitated by another voice. Any one endowed with normal powers of speech can imitate a markedly nasal speaking voice. This is equally true of a nasal tone in singing, and of a strongly throaty tone as well. The more marked the fault of production the more readily it is heard and the more easily it can be imitated.

Let us imagine the case of a vocal teacher who undertakes to teach a gifted pupil by having the pupil imitate tones of faulty production, and gradually correcting the faults in the tones sung as a model for the pupil. The master is of course understood to have perfect command of his own voice. Suppose this master to begin the course of instruction by singing for the pupil tones of exaggerated throaty quality, and bidding the pupil to imitate these tones. Naturally, the pupil would have no difficulty in doing so. At the next lesson the master would very slightly improve the quality of the tones sung as a model for the pupil's imitation. The student would listen to these tones and model his daily practice accordingly. Just so soon as the student had succeeded in correctly reproducing this slightly less throaty tone the master would again set a slightly improved model.

With each successive step the master might eliminate, one by one, the faults of his own tone-production. Following the same course, the pupil would also gradually approach a correct model of tone. Finally, all the faults of tone-production having been corrected, both of master and pupil, the latter would be called upon to imitate perfect vocal tones. It would necessarily follow either that the student would successfully imitate the master's perfect tones or that at some point in this progress the student's imitative faculty would be found lacking.

Could any point be located at which the student would be unable to imitate the teacher's voice? This could certainly not be in the early stages of the course. Any one can imitate a very bad throaty or nasal tone. This being done, the imitation of a slightly less faulty tone would also present no difficulty. A second improvement in the master's model tone would again be readily imitated, and so on, with each succeeding correction of the faults of production. When the last trace of faulty production in the student's voice had been eliminated, he would be singing perfect tones. It is utterly impossible to define a point in this progress at which the pupil would be unable to imitate the teacher's voice. If a bad fault of production can be imitated, so can a comparatively slight fault. Further, if the pupil can correct his pronounced faulty production by imitating a tone not quite so faulty, so can he improve upon this tone by imitating a still better model of production. This process of gradual improvement by imitation must be capable of continuation until the last fault is eliminated. No limit can be set to the ability of the voice to improve its manner of tone-production by imitation. It must therefore be concluded that the perfect vocal action can be acquired by imitation.

In practical Voice Culture, learning to sing by imitation means simply the cultivation of the sense of hearing and the guidance of the voice by the ear. In other words, those vocal theorists who insist upon ear training commit themselves to the theory of imitative Voice Culture. What necessity is there of mechanical management of the vocal organs if the voice is to be guided by the ear? Even if mechanical management of the voice were possible it would be entirely superfluous. The voice needs no other guidance than the singer's sense of hearing.

Here another striking question is encountered: Why should the vocal organs be thought to be unable to adjust themselves for the tone quality demanded by the ear any more than for the pitch? No vocal theorist has ever thought to formulate rules for securing the tension of the vocal cords necessary for the desired pitch. This is always left to instinctive processes. No one would ever undertake to question the voice's ability to sing by imitation a note of any particular pitch. What valid reason can be given for denying the corresponding ability regarding tone quality?

Only one answer can be made to this question. The whole matter of mechanical vocal management rests on pure assumption. No scientific proof has ever been sought for the belief that the voice requires mechanical management. This necessity is always assumed, but the assumption is utterly illogical. The vocal organs adjust themselves for the imitation of tone quality by exactly the same psychological processes as for the imitation of pitch.

Neither pitch nor tone quality can be regulated in any other way than by the guidance of the ear.

Imitation furnishes the only means of acquiring the correct vocal action. Several authorities on the voice admit the value of imitation, even though they also make much of the mechanical doctrines of modern methods. Sieber gives imitation as the best means of curing faults of production. "The best means to free the student of the three forms of faulty tone just described is possessed by that teacher who is able to imitate these faults with his own voice." (Vollst 鋘 diges Lehrbuch der Gesangskunst, Ferd. Sieber, 1858.) Dr. Mills goes further and advocates the imitating of finished singers for the purpose of acquiring the correct vocal action. "The author would recommend all students who have begun a serious practical study of the registers to hear, if possible, some singer of eminence who observes register formation strictly." (Voice Production in Singing and Speaking, Phila., 1906.) Kofler even declares that imitation is an indispensable element of instruction. "It is just as difficult or impossible to learn to sing good tones without hearing the teacher's pure model tone as it is difficult or impossible to learn to speak without hearing." (The Art of Breathing, Leo Kofler, 1889.)

If the correct vocal action is to be acquired by imitation, of what use are the mechanical doctrines of vocal management? Kofler seeks to combine these two forms of instruction. "Physiological theories must go hand in hand with the musical ear or the law of imitation." Scientifically considered, this attempted combination of mechanical vocal training and instruction by imitation is an utter absurdity. There is no possibility of connection between vocal imitation and mechanical vocal management. Reliance on the imitative faculty involves the utter rejection of the mechanical idea. Compromise, or combination of the two, is a logical absurdity. Imitation and attempted mechanical management of the voice are absolutely incompatible. Any attempt consciously to direct the muscular workings of the vocal organs is an interference with the normal action of the voice. So soon as conscious mechanical management of the voice is attempted throat stiffness results, and the voice is hampered in the exercise of its instinctive faculty of imitation. It is impossible to acquire the correct vocal action by the application of mechanical rules, because a consistent following of mechanical doctrines utterly prevents the vocal organs from operating normally, even though the student try at the same time to guide the voice by the sense of hearing.

A close scrutiny of the practices of modern vocal teachers reveals convincing evidence that all their successes are due to a reliance, conscious or unconscious, on the imitative faculty. Teachers are as a rule not aware of the appeal to the instinct of imitation; neither indeed do the students usually pay much attention to this feature of their lessons. Much of modern vocal instruction is dual in character. When, for example, the teacher wishes to correct a marked fault in the pupil's tone-production, he adopts this dual mode of imparting his ideas. First, he explains to the pupil the (supposed) mechanical operation; second, he imitates the pupil's faulty production and then sings a correct tone to show how it should be produced.

For the teacher to sing the correct tone takes but a few seconds and requires almost no thought. The mechanical explanation, on the other hand, calls for much more of time, and of voluntary attention, from both master and student. It thus follows that they both look upon the mechanical rule as the important matter, and consider the teacher's perfect tone as merely an illustration of the rule.

In most cases the student strives to apply the mechanical rule, particularly in home practice between lessons. Under these circumstances the voice does not respond satisfactorily. But it often happens that the student pays little attention to the mechanical rule, and simply imitates the teacher's voice. There being then nothing to interfere, the student's voice naturally responds. The master ascribes this satisfactory result to the application of the mechanical doctrine, while in fact the result is due to the student's complete ignoring of the doctrine.

Vocal imitation is often completely unconscious. Individuals vary greatly, as regards the tendency to unconscious imitation. Of two English lads coming to America at the age of fifteen, one may be found ten years later to have entirely lost the English accent, the other may retain it all his life. This difference in individual traits has much to do with determining to what extent the vocal student may unconsciously imitate correct models of singing. Other characteristics are also influential in this regard. Some students so dislike to sing mechanically that they neglect, in their home study, to practise their exercises in the prescribed way. This is often due to an instinctive abhorrence of harsh sounds. Other students are so gifted with the true feeling for vocal melody that mechanical instruction makes no impression on them.

As a general rule, the reliance on the imitative faculty in modern vocal instruction is entirely unconscious on the part of both master and pupil. Adherence to the mechanical idea excludes from the student's mind all thought of any means of vocal guidance other than mechanical. This is true, even in the most common form of instruction, imitation and mechanical doctrine combined. As regards the master, his only conscious exercise of the imitative faculty is the reproduction of the pupil's faulty tones. He seldom thinks of telling the pupil to imitate his own correctly produced tones.

Imitation supplies the only practical means for training voices. All the elements of Voice Culture are combined in one simple process, when the master sings correctly, and the student imitates the master. This exercise of the imitative faculty may be made to suffice for both the training of the ear and the cultivation of the voice. On practical, as well as on scientific grounds, imitation is the only rational basis of a method of Voice Culture.

CHAPTER VI

THE OLD ITALIAN METHOD

To the believer in the necessity of direct mechanical management of the voice, the old Italian method is a complete mystery. Modern vocal theorists are at a loss to account for the success of the old masters in training voices. Many authorities go so far as to assert that these masters possessed some insight into the operations of the vocal organs, along the lines of accepted Vocal Science. In their introductory chapter, "A Plea for Vocal Physiology," Browne and Behnke attempt to prove that the old masters studied the anatomy of the vocal organs. But even if this could be proved, that would not solve the mystery of the old method. Modern teachers are certainly as well acquainted with the mechanical features of tone-production as the old masters were. Yet, judged by their results, modern methods are distinctly inferior to the old Italian method.

There is absolutely no ground for the belief that the old masters owed their success to a knowledge of vocal physiology. This idea of ascribing scientific knowledge to the early teachers results only from erroneous belief that no other means of training the voice is possible. It may be set down as absolutely certain that the old method was not based on the principles of the accepted Vocal Science.

Yet the old masters undoubtedly possessed some means of training voices. They must have known something about the voice. Their knowledge, whatever it was, is commonly believed to have been lost. Many modern teachers claim to have inherited the old method. Still these teachers have nothing to offer beyond the well-known doctrines of breathing, breath-control, forward tone, etc. How these doctrines might have been applied in practical instruction nobody is able to tell. Little attention need be paid to the claim of any modern teacher to possess the old Italian method of training voices.

So early as 1847 Garcia remarked the dearth of information of a literary character bearing on the old method. "Unfortunately this epoch has left us only vague and incomplete documents bearing on its traditions. Of the methods then followed we have only an approximate and confused idea." (蓋 ole de Garcia, Mayence, 1847.) Although familiar with the works of Tosi and Mancini, Garcia was unable to find in their writings any hint of the means used for imparting the correct vocal action. This same remark is made by many other investigators.

Yet a reconstruction of the old method is not necessarily a matter of conjecture. Once the possibility of training the voice by imitation is established, the old Italian method is easily understood. Speaking of the glorious past of the art of Voice Culture, Dr. Mills says: "We have advanced, musically, in many respects since the days of the old Italian masters, but just as we must turn to the Greeks to learn what constitutes the highest and best in sculpture, so must we sit at the feet of these old masters. Consciously or unconsciously they taught on sound physiological principles." (Voice Production in Singing and Speaking.)

Dr. Mills' statement might be more complete if it were made to read, "consciously or unconsciously they taught on sound physiological and psychological principles." Vocal instruction on sound principles is simply the training of the voice by imitation. With the scientific basis of their method-- the laws of physiological psychology--the old masters were utterly unacquainted. Vocal imitation is purely instinctive. Probably the old masters could not even have formulated a concise statement of their reasons for relying on the imitative faculty.

Garcia's complaint of the dearth of literary information regarding the old method is by no means justified. Naturally there is no record of any means for imparting a direct mechanical management of the voice. Nothing of the kind was thought of. But as a description of a course in voice training by imitation, the works of Tosi and Mancini leave little to be desired.

Both Tosi and Mancini devote by far the greater portion of their books to describing the ornaments and embellishments of vocal music. They take up the singer's education from the beginning and seem to assume, as a matter of course, that the training in the art of music is coincident, if not indeed identical, with the cultivation of the voice. But they do not by any means neglect the subject of tone-production. Most modern readers of these early writers overlook the simple directions given for securing a proper use of the voice. This is, of course, due to the current belief that directions for vocal management must of necessity deal with mechanical and muscular operations. Finding nothing of this kind in Tosi and Mancini, the modern investigator concludes that these writers for some reason failed to record the means used for imparting the correct vocal action. All that can be found by such an investigator in the works of Tosi and Mancini is an outline of an elaborate system of coloratura singing. Much more is seen when the meaning of imitative Voice Culture is understood.

Let us consider first the "Observations" of Tosi. This writer devotes his first few pages to some remarks on the art of singing, and to a general consideration of the practices of Voice Culture. Almost at the outset we meet this striking statement: "It would be needless to say that verbal instruction would be of no use to singers any farther than to prevent 'em falling into errors, and that it is practice alone can set them right." That is certainly a sound principle.

Consider also this passage. "The faults in singing insinuate themselves so easily into the minds of young beginners, and there are such difficulties in correcting them, when grown into an habit, that it were to be wished the ablest singers would undertake the task of teaching, they best knowing how to conduct the scholar from the first elements to perfection. But there being none (if I mistake not) but who abhor the thoughts of it, we must reserve them for those delicacies of the art, which enchant the soul. Therefore the first rudiments necessarily fall to a master of a lower rank, till the scholar can sing his part at sight; whom one would at least wish to be an honest man, diligent and experienced, without the defects of singing through the nose, or in the throat, and that he have a command of voice, some glimpse of a good taste, able to make himself understood with ease, a perfect intonation, and a patience to endure the fatigue of a most tiresome employment."

This brings out three striking facts. First, that the student learned to use his voice by imitating the voice of the master. Second, that the initial work of "voice placing" was merely an incident in the training in sight singing and the rudiments of music. Third, that "voice placing" was considered of too little importance to claim the attention of masters of the first rank. This feature of instruction, so important now as to overshadow all else, was at that time left to masters of a lower rank.

This passage is followed by a short discourse on the rudiments of Sol Fa, a subject of only academic interest to the modern student. We are so thoroughly accustomed nowadays to the diatonic scale that it is almost impossible for us to understand the old system of Muance or Solmisation. Suffice it to say that only four keys were known, and that each note was called by its full Sol-Fa name. Thus D was called D-la-sol-re, C was C-sol-fa-ut, etc. In studying sight singing, the student pronounced the full name of each note in every exercise. Instruction in singing began with this study of sight reading. In the course of this practice the student somehow learned to produce his voice correctly.

Tosi does not leave us in doubt what was to be done in order to lead the pupil to adopt a correct manner of tone-production. "Let the master do his utmost to make the scholar hit and sound the notes perfectly in tune in Sol-Fa-ing.... Let the master attend with great care to the voice of the scholar, which should always come forth neat and clear, without passing through the nose or being choaked in the throat." To sing in tune and to produce tones of good quality,--this summed up for Tosi the whole matter of tone-production.

Many teachers in the old days composed Sol-Fa exercises and vocalises for their own use. Tosi did not think this indispensable. But he points out the need of the teacher having an extensive repertoire of graded exercises and vocalises. To his mind these should always be melodious and singable. "If the master does not understand composition let him provide himself with good examples of Sol-Fa-ing in divers stiles, which insensibly lead from the most easy to the most difficult, according as he finds the scholar improves; with this caution, that however difficult, they may be always natural and agreeable, to induce the scholar to study with pleasure."

How many months of study were supposed to be required for this preliminary course we have no means of judging from Tosi's work. At any rate the combining of the registers was accomplished during this time. Tosi's description of the registers is very concise. "Voce di Petto is a full voice which comes from the breast by strength, and is the most sonorous and expressive. Voce di Testa comes more from the throat than from the breast, and is capable of more volubility. Falsetto is a feigned voice which is formed entirely in the throat, has more volubility than any, but of no substance." He speaks of the necessity of uniting the registers, but gives no directions how this is to be accomplished. Evidently this seemed to him to present no difficulty whatever.

In this early period of instruction the pupil was exercised in both portamento and messa di voce. "Let him learn the manner to glide with the vowels, and to drag the voice gently from the high to the lower note.... In the same lessons let him teach the art to put forth the voice, which consists in letting it swell by degrees from the softest Piano to the loudest Forte, and from thence with the same art return from the Forte to the Piano. A beautiful Messa di Voce can never fail of having an excellent effect."

Only the first chapter of Tosi's book is devoted to this initial study. That the student was expected to make steady progress as a result of this study is evident from the closing sentence of this chapter. "The scholar having now made some remarkable progress, the instructor may acquaint him with the first embellishments of the art, which are the Appoggiaturas, and apply them to the vowels." The remainder of the work is devoted almost entirely to the embellishments of singing. Here and there an interesting passage is found. "After the scholar has made himself perfect in the Shake and the Divisions, the master should let him read and pronounce the words." (Shake was the old name for trill, and division for run.) Again, "I return to the master only to put him in mind that his duty is to teach musick; and if the scholar, before he gets out of his hands, does not sing readily and at sight, the innocent is injured without remedy from the guilty." This injunction might well be taken to heart by the modern teacher. Good sight readers are rare nowadays, outside of chorus choirs.

Mancini begins his outline of the course of instruction in singing with this striking sentence: "Nothing is more insufferable and more inexcusable in a musician than wrong intonation; singing in the throat or in the nose will certainly be tolerated rather than singing out of tune." This is followed by the advice to the teacher to ascertain beyond a doubt that a prospective pupil is endowed with a true musical ear. This being done the pupil is to begin his studies by sol-fa-ing the scales. "Having determined the disposition and capacity of the student with respect to intonation, and finding him able and disposed to succeed, let him fortify himself in correct intonation by sol-fa-ing the scale, ascending and descending. This must be executed with scrupulous attention in order that the notes may be perfectly intoned."

In this practice the quality of the tone is of the highest importance. "The utmost care is necessary with the student to render him able to manage this portion of his voice with the proper sweetness and proportion." Mancini takes it for granted that the student will progress steadily on account of this practice. "When the teacher observes that the pupil is sufficiently free in delivering the voice, in intonation, and in naming the notes, let him waste no time, but have the pupil vocalize without delay."

Regarding the registers, Mancini disagrees with Tosi and names only two. "Voices ordinarily divide themselves into two registers which are called, one of the chest, the other of the head, or falsetto." His method was to exercise the voice at first in the chest register, and then gradually to extend the compass of the voice upward. "Every student can for himself with perfect ease recognize the difference between these two separate registers. It will suffice therefore to commence by singing the scale, for example, if a soprano, from G to d;[10] let him take care that these five notes are sonorous, and say them with force and clearness, and without effort." For uniting the registers, "the most certain means is to hold back the tones of the chest and to sing the transition notes in the head register, increasing the power little by little."

[Note 10: Mancini of course uses the Sol-Fa names of these notes.]

Mancini devotes a few pages to a description of the vocal organs. This fact is cited by several modern theorists in support of their statement that the old masters based their methods on mechanical principles. In the following chapter this topic of Mancini's treatise will be considered.

Probably the best summary of the old Italian method offered by any modern teacher is contained in a little booklet by J. Frank Botume, entitled Modern Singing Methods. (Boston, 1885. The citations are from the fourth edition, 1896.) Speaking of the meaning of the word method, as applied to a system of rules for acquiring the correct vocal action, this writer says: "If a teacher says, 'that tone is harsh, sing more sweetly,' he has given no method to his pupil. He has asked the scholar to change his tone, but has not shown him how to do it. If, on the other hand, he directs the pupil to keep back the pressure of the breath, or to change the location of the tone; if he instructs him in regard to the correct use of his vocal cords, or speaks of the position of his tongue, of his diaphragm, of his mouth, etc., he gives him method. The Italian teachers of the early period of this art had so little method that it can hardly be said to have existed with them. In fact, the word method, as now used, is of comparatively modern origin. The founders of the art of singing aimed at results directly; the manner of using the vocal apparatus for the purpose of reaching these results troubled them comparatively little. The old Italian teacher took the voice as he found it. He began with the simplest and easiest work, and trusted to patient and long-continued exercise to develop the vocal apparatus. In all this there is no method as we understand the term. The result is aimed at directly. The manner of getting it is not shown. There is no conscious control of the vocal apparatus for the purpose of effecting a certain result."

This sums up beautifully the external aspects of the old Italian method, and of modern methods as well. It points out clearly the difference between the old and the modern system. But it is a mistake to say that the old masters followed no systematized plan of instruction. Tosi's advice, already quoted ("Let the master provide himself with examples of Sol-fa, leading insensibly from the easy to the difficult," etc.), shows a thorough grasp of the meaning of methodical instruction. Once the real nature of vocal training is understood, both Tosi and Mancini are seen to describe a well worked out system of Voice Culture. The only important difference between the old and the new system is this: one relied on instinctive and imitative processes for imparting the correct vocal action, the other seeks to accomplish the same result through the mechanical management of the vocal organs. In this regard the advantage is all on the side of the old Italian method.

One question regarding the old method remains to be answered. This has to do with the use of the empirical precepts in practical instruction. So far as the written record goes we have no means of answering this question. Neither Tosi nor Mancini mentions the old precepts in any way. The answer can therefore be only conjectural. We may at once dismiss the idea that the old masters used the precepts in the currently accepted manner as rules for the mechanical management of the voice. This application of the empirical precepts followed upon the acceptance of the idea of mechanical voice culture.

A fine description of perfect singing, considered empirically, was found to be embodied in the traditional precepts. Such a description of correctly produced tone might be of great value in the training of the ear. The sense of hearing is developed by listening; and attentive listening is rendered doubly effective in the singer's education by the attention being consciously directed to particular characteristics of the sounds observed.

A highly important aspect of ear training in Voice Culture is the acquainting the student with the highest standards of singing. The student derives a double advantage from listening to artistic singing when he knows what to listen for. Telling the student that in perfect singing the throat seems to be open makes him keenly attentive in observing this characteristic sound of the correctly produced tone. This seems to be the most effective manner of utilizing the empirical precepts. A student may be helped in imitating correct models of singing by knowing what characteristics of the tones it is most important to reproduce. In pointing out to the student his own faults of production, the judicious use of the precepts might also be of considerable value. Probably the old masters treated the precepts about in this fashion.

CHAPTER VII

THE DISAPPEARANCE OF THE OLD ITALIAN METHOD AND THE

DEVELOPMENT OF MECHANICAL INSTRUCTION

One of the most mysterious facts in the history of Voice Culture is the utter disappearance of the old Italian method. This has occurred in spite of the earnest efforts of vocal teachers to preserve the old traditions. If the conclusions drawn in the preceding chapter are justified, the old method consisted of a system of teaching singing by imitation. Assuming this to be true, there should now be no difficulty in accounting for the disappearance of the imitative method by tracing the development of the mechanical idea.

Imitative Voice Culture was purely empirical in the ordinary meaning of this word. The old masters did not knowingly base their instruction on any set of principles. They simply taught as their instincts prompted them. There can now be no doubt that the old masters were fully justified in their empiricism. They taught singing as Nature intends it to be taught. But the old masters were not aware of the scientific soundness of their position. So soon as the correctness of empirical teaching was questioned they abandoned it without an attempt at defense. As a system of Voice Culture, the old method occupied a weak strategic position. With absolute right on its side, it still had no power of resistance against hostile influences.

This does not imply that the old masters were ignorant men. On the contrary, the intellectual standard of the vocal profession seems to have been fully as high two hundred years ago as to-day. Even famous composers and musical theorists did not disdain to teach singing. But this very fact, the generally high culture of the old masters, was an important factor in the weakness of the old method against attack. The most intelligent masters were the ones most likely to abandon the empirical system in favor of supposedly scientific and precise methods of instruction.

The hostile influence to which the old Italian method succumbed was the idea of mechanical vocal management. This idea entered almost imperceptibly into the minds of vocal teachers in the guise of a scientific theory of Voice Culture. A short historical sketch will bring this fact out clearly. This necessitates a repetition of some of the material of Chapter I of

Part I; the entire subject will however appear

in a new light now that the true nature of the mechanical idea is understood.

From the founding of the art of Voice Culture, about 1600, up to 1741, no vocalist seems to have paid any attention to the anatomy or muscular movements of the vocal organs. In 1741 a French physician, Ferrein, presented to the Academy of Sciences a treatise on the anatomy of the vocal organs, entitled "De la Formation de la Voix de l'Homme." This treatise was published in the same year, and it seems to have attracted at once the attention of the most enlightened masters of singing. That Ferrein was the first to call the attention of vocalists to the mechanical features of tone-production is strongly indicated in the German translation of Tosi's "Observations." In the original Italian edition, 1723, and the English translation, 1742, there is absolutely no mention of the anatomy or physiology of the vocal organs. But in preparing the German edition, published in 1757, the translator, J. F. Agricola, inserted a description of the vocal organs which he credited directly to Ferrein.

Mancini followed Agricola's example, and included in this "Riflessioni" (1776) a brief description of the vocal organs. But Mancini made no attempt to apply this description in formulating a system of instruction. He recommends the parents of a prospective singer to ascertain, by a physician's examination, that the child's vocal organs are normal and in good health. He also gives one mechanical rule, so obvious as to seem rather quaint. "Every singer must place his mouth in a natural smiling position, that is, with the upper teeth perpendicularly and moderately removed from the lower." Beyond this Mancini says not a word of mechanical vocal management. There is no mention of breathing, or tone reflection, or laryngeal action. Although Mancini borrowed his description of the vocal organs from Ferrein, his notion of the mechanics of tone-production was very crude. "The air of the lungs operates on the larynx in singing exactly as it operates on the head of the flute."

Voice Culture has passed through three successive periods. From 1600 to 1741 instruction in singing was purely empirical. Ferrein's treatise may be said to mark the beginning of a transition period during which empirical instruction was gradually displaced by so-called scientific methods. This transition period lasted, roughly speaking, till the invention of the laryngoscope in 1855. Since that time vocal instruction has been carried on almost exclusively along mechanical lines.

No vocal teacher had ever heard of a problem of tone-production previous to 1741, and indeed for many years thereafter. The earlier masters were not aware of any possibility of difficulty in causing the voice to operate properly. Their success justified their ignoring of any mechanical basis of instruction; but even of this justification the later masters of the old school were only dimly conscious. They builded better than they knew. When any teacher of the transition period was called upon to explain his manner of imparting the correct vocal action he was at once put on the defensive. No champion of the imitative faculty could be found. This lack of understanding of the basis of the empirical method, on the part of its most intelligent and successful exponents, was the first cause of the weakness of this method against attack.

Another source of weakness in the hold of empirical systems on the vocal profession was seen in the generally high intellectual standard of the more prominent teachers. These masters gladly accepted the new knowledge of the basis of their art, offered them in the description of the vocal organs. Thoroughly conversant with every detail of the empirical knowledge of the voice, the masters of the transition period were well prepared to understand something of the mechanical features of tone-production. By their auditory and muscular sensations of vocal tone they were able, to their own satisfaction at least, to verify the statements of the anatomists.

It is not easy for us to put ourselves mentally in the position of a vocalist, thoroughly familiar with the empirical knowledge of the voice, and yet ignorant of the first principles of vocal mechanics. In all probability the early masters were not even aware that tone is produced by the action of the breath on the larynx. They did not know that different qualities and pitches result from special adjustments and contractions of the throat muscles. Yet they were keenly aware of all the muscular sensations resulting from these contractions. We can well imagine how interesting these vocalists of the early transition period must have found the description of the cartilages and muscles of the throat.

It seems to us but a short step from the study of vocal mechanics to the application of the results of this study in the formulating of a practical system of vocal instruction. Yet it required more than sixty years for the vocal profession to travel so far. Even then the true bearing of this development of Voice Culture was but dimly realized. In 1800 the mechanical management of the voice was not even thought of. This is conclusively proved by a most important work, the M閏hode de Chant du Conservatoire de Musique, published in Paris in 1803.

There can be no question that this Mehode represents the most enlightened and advanced thought of the vocal profession of that day. Not only does it contain everything then known about the training of the voice; it was drawn up with the same exhaustive care and analytical attention to detail that were devoted to the formulation of the metric system. To mechanical rules less than one page is devoted. Respiration is the only subject to receive more than a few lines. A system of breathing with flat abdomen and high chest is outlined, and the student is instructed to practise breathing exercises daily. Five lines are contained in the chapter headed "De l'emission du son," and these five lines are simply a warning against throaty and nasal quality. The pupil is told to stand erect, and to open the mouth properly. But a foot-note is given to the rule for the position of the mouth which shows how thoroughly the mechanical rule was subordinated to considerations of tone quality. "As there is no rule without exceptions, we think it useful to observe at what opening of the mouth the pupil produces the most agreeable, sonorous, and pure quality of tone in order to have him always open the mouth in that manner." In the main the M閏hode outlines a purely empirical system of instruction, based on the guidance of the voice by the ear. There can be no question that the idea of mechanical management of the voice was introduced later than 1803.

Citations might be made to show the gradual advance of the mechanical idea from two interesting works, Die Kunst des Gesanges, by Adolph B. Marx, Berlin, 1826, and Die grosse italienische Gesangschule, by H. F. Mannstein, Dresden, 1834. But this is not necessary. It is enough to say that Scientific Voice Culture was not generally thought to be identical with mechanical vocal management until later than 1855.

Manuel Garcia was the first vocal teacher to undertake to found a practical method of instruction on the mechanical principles of the vocal action. When only twenty-seven years old, in 1832, Garcia determined to reform the practices of Voice Culture by furnishing an improved method of instruction.

(Grove's Dictionary.) His first definite pronouncement of this purpose is contained in the preface to his de Garcia, 1847. "As all the effects of song are, in the last analysis, the product of the vocal organs, I have submitted the study to physiological considerations." This statement of Garcia's idea of scientific instruction strikes us as a commonplace. But that serves only to prove how thoroughly the world has since been converted to the idea of mechanical Voice Culture. At that time it was generally believed to be a distinct advance. Garcia expected to bring about a great improvement in the art of Voice Culture. His idea was that the voice can be trained in less time and with greater certainty by mechanical than by imitative methods. As for the inherent falsity of this idea, that has been sufficiently exposed.

So soon as the theory of mechanical vocal management began to find acceptance, the old method yielded the ground to the new idea. That this occurred so easily was due to a number of causes. Of these several have already been noted,--the readiness of the most prominent teachers to broaden their field of knowledge, in particular. Other causes contributing to the acceptance of the mechanical idea were the elusive character of empirical knowledge of the voice, and the unconscious aspect of the instinct of vocal imitation. No master of the later transition period deliberately discarded his empirical knowledge. This could have been possible only by the master losing his sense of hearing. Neither did the master cease to rely on the imitative faculty. Although unconsciously exercised, that was a habit too firmly fixed to be even intentionally abandoned.

Public opinion also had much to do with the spread of the mechanical idea. Teachers found that they could get pupils easier by claiming to understand the mechanical workings of the voice. In order to obtain recognition, teachers were obliged to study vocal mechanics and to adapt their methods to the growing demand for scientific instruction.

No master of this period seems to have intentionally abandoned the traditional method. Their first purpose in adopting the new scientific idea was to elucidate and fortify the old method. Every successful master undoubtedly taught many pupils who in their turn became teachers. There must have been, in each succession of master and pupil, one teacher who failed to transmit the old method in its entirety. Both master and pupil must have been unconscious of this. No master can be believed to have deliberately withheld any of his knowledge from his pupils. Neither can any student have been aware that he failed to receive his master's complete method.

Let us consider a typical instance of master and pupil in the later transition period. Instruction in this case was probably of a dual character. Both teacher and pupil devoted most of their attention to the mechanical features of tone-production. Yet the master continued to listen closely to the student's voice, just as he had done before adopting the (supposedly) scientific idea of instruction. Unconsciously he led the pupil to listen and imitate. When the student found it difficult to apply the mechanical instruction the master would say, "Listen to me and do as I do." Naturally this would bring the desired result. Yet both master and pupil would attribute the result to the application of the mechanical rule. The student's voice would be successfully trained, but he would carry away an erroneous idea of the means by which this was accomplished. Becoming a teacher in his turn, the vocalist taught in this fashion would entirely overlook the unobtrusive element of imitation and would devote himself to mechanical instruction. He would, for example, construe the precept, "Sing with open throat," as a rule to be directly applied; that he had acquired the open throat by imitating his master's tones this teacher would be utterly unaware.

More than one generation of master and pupil was probably concerned, in each succession, in the gradual loss of the substance of the old method. The possibility of learning to sing by imitation was only gradually lost to sight. This is well expressed by Paolo Guetta. "The aphorism 'listen and imitate,' which was the device of the ancient school, coming down by way of tradition, underwent the fate of all sane precepts passed along from generation to generation. Through elimination and individual adaptation, through assuming the personal imprint, it degenerated into a purely empirical formula." (Il Canto nel suo Mecanismo, Milan, 1902.)

Guetta is himself evidently at a loss to grasp the significance of the empirical formula, "Listen and imitate." He seems however to be aware of an antagonism between imitation and mechanical vocal management. The reason of this antagonism has already been noticed, but it will bear repetition. For a teacher to tell a pupil to "hold your throat open and imitate my tone," is to demand the impossible. A conscious effort directly to hold the throat open only causes the throat to stiffen. In this condition the normal action of the voice is upset and the pupil cannot imitate the teacher's voice.

This was the condition confronting the teacher of the second generation in the "maestral succession" just considered. He found his pupils unable to get with their voices the results which had come easily to him. Attributing his satisfactory progress as a student to the mastery of the supposed mechanical principles of tone-production, this teacher ascribed his pupil's difficulties to their failure to grasp the same mechanical ideas. As a natural consequence he labored even more energetically along mechanical lines. Curiously, no teacher seems to have questioned the soundness of the mechanical idea. Failure on the part of the pupil to obtain the correct use of the voice served only to make the master more insistent on mechanical exercises.

In direct proportion to the prominence given to the idea of mechanical management of the voice, the difficulties of teachers and students became ever more pronounced. The trouble caused by throat stiffness led the teachers to seek new means for imparting the correct vocal action, always along mechanical lines. In this way the progress of the mechanical idea was accelerated, and the problem of tone-production received ever more attention.

Faith in the imitative faculty was gradually undermined by the progress of the mechanical idea. With each succeeding generation of master and pupil, the mechanical idea became more firmly established. Something akin to a vicious circle was involved in this progress. As attention was paid in practical instruction to the mechanical operations of the voice, so the voice's instinctive power of imitation was curtailed by throat stiffness. This served to make more pressing the apparent need of means for the mechanical management of the voice. Thus the mechanical idea found ever new arguments in its favor, based always on the difficulties itself had caused.

It is impossible to assign a precise date to the disappearance of the old Italian method. The last exponent of the old traditions was Francesco Lamperti, who retired from active teaching in 1876. Yet even Lamperti finally yielded, in theory at least, to the mechanical idea. In the closing years of his active life as a teacher (1875 and 1876), Lamperti wrote a book descriptive of his method, A Treatise on the Art of Singing (translated into English by J. C. Griffith and published by Ed. Schuberth & Co., New York). When this work was about ready for the press, Lamperti read Dr. Mandl's Gesundheitslehre der Stimme, containing the first definite statement of the opposed-muscular-action theory of breath-control. At the last moment Lamperti inserted a note in his book to signify his acceptance of this theory.

Vocal mechanics was at first studied by teachers of singing as a matter of purely academic interest. No insufficiency of imitative teaching had ever been felt. Teachers of the transition period, even so late probably as 1830, had in most cases no reason to be dissatisfied with their methods of instruction. Garcia himself started out modestly enough to place the traditional method, received from his father, on a definite basis. His first idea, announced in the preface to the first edition of his 蓋 ole de Garcia, was to "reproduce my father's method, attempting only to give it a more theoretical form, and to connect results with causes."

Interest in the mechanics of the voice continued to be almost entirely academic until the invention of the laryngoscope in 1855. Then the popular note was struck. The marvelous industrial and scientific progress of the preceding fifty years had prepared the world to demand advancement in methods of teaching singing, as in everything else. When the secrets of the vocal action were laid bare, a new and better method of teaching singing was at once expected. Within very few years scientific knowledge of the voice was demanded of every vocal teacher.

Nothing could well be more natural than a belief in the efficacy of scientific knowledge of the vocal organs as the basis of instruction in singing. Surely no earnest investigator of the voice can be criticized for adopting this belief. No one ever thought of questioning the soundness of the new scientific idea. The belief was everywhere accepted, as a matter of course, that methods of instruction in singing were about to be vastly improved. Vocal theorists spoke confidently of discovering means for training the voice in a few months of study. The singer's education under the old system had demanded from four to seven years; science was expected to revolutionize this, and to accomplish in months what had formerly required years.

Even then tone-production was not seen to be a distinct problem. The old imitative method was still successfully followed. No one thought of discarding the traditional method, but only of improving it by reducing it to scientific principles. But that could not last. Soon after the attempt began to be made to manage the voice mechanically, tone-production was found to contain a real problem. This was of course due to the introduction of throat stiffness.

From that time on (about 1860 to 1865), the problem of tone-production has become steadily more difficult of solution in each individual case. This problem has been, since 1865, the one absorbing topic of Voice Culture. Probably the most unfortunate single fact in the history of Voice Culture is that scientific study of the voice was from the beginning confined solely to the mechanical features of tone-production. Had scientific investigators turned their attention also to the analysis of the auditory impressions of vocal tones, and to the psychological aspect of tone-production, scientific instruction in singing would probably not have been identified with mechanical management of the voice. All the subsequent difficulties of the vocal profession would almost certainly have been avoided.

Every attempt at a solution of the problem of tone-production has been made along strictly mechanical lines. Attention has been devoted solely to the anatomy and physiology of the vocal organs, and to the acoustic principles of the vocal action. Since 1865 hardly a year has passed without some important contribution to the sum of knowledge of the vocal mechanism. For many years this development of Vocal Science was eagerly followed by the vocal teachers. Any seemingly authoritative announcement of a new theory of the voice was sure to bring its reward in an immediate influx of earnest students. Prominent teachers made it their practice to spend their vacations in studying with the famous specialists and investigators. Each new theory of the vocal action was at once put into practice, or at any rate this attempt was made. Yet each new attempt brought only a fresh disappointment. The mystery of the voice was only deepened with each successive failure at solution.

A review in detail of the development of Vocal Science would be of only academic interest. Very little of practical moment would probably be added to the outline of modern methods contained in

Part I.

Teachers of singing at present evince an attitude of skepticism toward new theories of the vocal action. Voice Culture has settled along well-established lines. In the past fifteen years little change can be noted in the practices of vocal teachers. The mechanical idea is so firmly established that no question is ever raised as to its scientific soundness. Under the limitations imposed by this erroneous idea, teachers do their best to train the voices entrusted to their care.

Vocal Science is of vastly less importance in modern Voice Culture than the world in general supposes. Only an imaginary relation has ever existed between the scientific knowledge of the voice and practical methods of instruction. To cause the summits of the arytenoid cartilages, for example, to incline toward each other is entirely beyond the direct power of the singer. How many similar impossibilities have been seriously advocated can be known only to the academic student of Vocal Science. Vocal teachers in general have ceased to attempt any such application of the doctrines of Vocal Science. Even if these doctrines could be shown to be scientifically sound it would still be impossible to devise means for applying them to the management of the voice. Accepted Vocal Science has contributed only one element of the practical scheme of modern voice culture; this is the erroneous notion that the vocal organs require to be managed mechanically.

CHAPTER VIII

THE MATERIALS OF RATIONAL INSTRUCTION IN SINGING

Practical methods of instruction in singing may be judged by their results fully as well as by a scientific analysis of their basic principles. If the progress of the art of singing in the past fifty years has been commensurate with the amount of study devoted to the operations of the vocal mechanism, then the value of present methods is established. Otherwise the need is proved for some reform in the present system of training voices. Judged by this standard modern methods are not found to be satisfactory. There has been no progress in the art of singing; exactly the contrary is the case. A prominent vocalist goes so far as to say that "vocal insufficiency and decay are prevalent." (The Singing of the Future, D. Frangen-Davies, M.A., 1906.) It is perhaps an exaggeration of the condition to call it "insufficiency and decay." Yet a gradual decline in the art of singing must be apparent to any lover of the art who has listened to most of the famous singers of the past twenty or twenty-five years. Operatic performance has been improved in every other respect, but pure singing, the perfection of the vocal art, has become almost a rarity. This is true not only of coloratura singing; it applies with almost equal force to the use of the singing voice for the purpose of dramatic and emotional expression.

Musical critics are beginning to comment on the decline of singing. They seek naturally for the causes of this decline. Many influences are cited by different writers, each of which has undoubtedly contributed something toward lowering the present standard of singing. Most influential among these contributing causes, in the general opinion, is the dramatic style of singing demanded in Wagner's later operas. Yet several writers point out that the roles of Tristan, Brunnhilde, etc., are vastly more effective when well sung than when merely shouted or declaimed. A change in the public taste is also spoken of. Audiences are said to be indifferent to the older operas, written to suit the style of florid singing. But even this statement does not pass unchallenged. A prominent critic asserts that "the world is still hungry" for florid singing. "It is altogether likely," continues this writer, "that composers would begin to write florid works again if they were assured of competent interpretation, for there is always a public eager for music of this sort." This critic asserts that the decline of coloratura singing is due to the indifference of the artists themselves to this style of singing.

Still another commentator ascribes the decline of pure singing in recent years to the rise of a new school of dramatic interpretation among the younger operatic artists. "Nowadays it is not the singing that counts. It is the interpretation; and the chances are there will be more and more interpretation and less and less singing every year." Even this view has its limitations. Faithful dramatic interpretation, and attention to all the details of make-up and "business," are not in any way antagonistic to pure singing. One of the most potent means of emotional expression is vocal tone color. But the skilful use of expressive tone quality is possible only to a singer possessed of a perfect command of all the resources of the voice. Many vocal shortcomings are forgiven in the singer of convincing interpretive power. This is probably an important factor in influencing the younger generation of artists to devote so much attention to interpretation.

More important than any of the reasons just given to account for the present state of the art of singing, is the decline in the art of training voices. The prospects of an improvement in the art of Voice Culture, imagined by the early investigators of the vocal mechanism, have not been realized. Voice Culture has not progressed in the past sixty years. Exactly the contrary has taken place. Before the introduction of mechanical methods every earnest vocal student was sure of learning to use his voice properly, and of developing the full measure of his natural endowments. Mechanical instruction has upset all this. Nowadays the successful vocal student is the exception. Even those students who succeed in acquiring sufficient command of their voices to win public acceptance are unable to master the finest points of vocal technique.

Perfect singing is becoming rare, mainly because the technical mastery of the voice cannot be acquired under modern methods of instruction. These methods have been found unsatisfactory in every way. A change must be made in the practices of Voice Culture; its present state cannot be regarded as permanent. Modern methods are not truly scientific. There is at present no justification for the belief that the art of Voice Culture is founded an assured scientific principles. This does not by any means invalidate the idea that Voice Culture is properly a subject for scientific regulation. Modern methods are unsatisfactory only because they do not conform to the fundamental laws of science. In order to erect a satisfactory art of Voice Culture it is necessary only that the art be brought into conformity with scientific principles.

No sweeping reform of modern methods is called for. A thorough application of scientific principles in the training of voices demands only one thing,--the abandonment of the idea of mechanical vocal management. This is not a backward step; on the contrary, it means a distinct advance. Once freed from the burden of the mechanical idea, the art of Voice Culture will be in position to advance, even beyond the ideals of the old masters.

Nothing could well be simpler than the dropping of the mechanical idea. It was pointed out in the review of modern methods that most of the time spent in giving and taking lessons is devoted to actual singing by the student. This is exactly what rational instruction means. Were it not for the evil influence of the mechanical idea, the results of present instruction would in most cases be satisfactory. It is only in consequence of the attention paid to the mechanical workings of the vocal organs that throat stiffness is interposed between the ear and the voice. Let the mechanical idea be dropped, and instruction may be carried on exactly as at present. There will be only one marked difference,--throat stiffness will cease to be a source of difficulty.

It is for the individual teacher to change his own practices. This could be done so easily that students would hardly note a change in the form of instruction. Simply call the pupil's attention always to the quality of the tones, and never to the throat. Cease to talk of breathing and of laryngeal action, and these subjects will never suggest themselves to the student's mind. Continue to have the student sing vocalises, scales, songs, and arias, just as at present. Teach the student to listen closely to his own voice, and familiarize him with correct models of singing. This covers the whole ground of rational Voice Culture.

It is a great mistake to suppose that a vocal student comes to the teacher with a definite idea of the need of direct vocal management. Several months of study are required before the student begins to grasp the teacher's idea of mechanical management of the voice. Even then the student rarely comes to a clear understanding of the mechanical idea. In the great majority of cases the student never gets beyond the vague notion that he must "do something" to bring the tones. Yet this vague idea is enough to keep his attention constantly directed to his vocal organs, and so to hamper their normal activity. So soon as a teacher drops the mechanical idea, his pupils will not think of their throats, nor demand mechanical instruction. There will be no need of his cautioning his pupils not to pay attention to the muscular workings of the vocal organs. No vocal student ever would do this were the practice not demanded in modern methods.

At first thought it may seem that for a teacher to drop all mechanical instruction would leave a great gap in his method. How is the correct vocal action to be imparted to the pupil if not by direct instruction to this end? This question has already been answered in preceding chapters, but the answer may well be repeated. The correct vocal action is naturally and instinctively adopted by the voice without any attention being paid to the operations of the vocal mechanism. It is necessary only that the student sing his daily exercises and listen to his voice. The voice's own instinct will lead it gradually to the perfect action. Nothing need be substituted for mechanical instruction.

Present methods of Voice Culture will be in every way complete, they will leave nothing to be desired, when the mechanical idea is abandoned. This change in the character of vocal instruction will not be in any sense a return to empiricism. It will be a distinct advance in the application of scientific principles.

When fully understood, a practical science of Voice Culture is seen to embrace only three topics,--the musical education of the student, the training of the ear, and the acquirement of skill in the use of the voice. The avoidance of throat stiffness is not properly a separate topic of Vocal Science, as in rational instruction nothing should ever be done to cause the throat to stiffen. Let us consider in detail these three topics of practical Vocal Science.

The Musical Education of a Singer

Every singer should be a well-educated and accomplished musician. This does not mean that the singer must be a capable performer on the piano or violin; yet some facility in playing the piano is of enormous benefit to the singer. A general understanding of the art of music is not necessarily dependent on the ability to play any instrument. The rudiments of music may quite well be mastered through the study of sight singing. This was the course adopted by the old masters, and it will serve equally well in our day.

One of the evil results of the introduction of the mechanical idea in Voice Culture is that almost the entire lesson time is devoted to the matter of tone-production. To the rudiments of music no attention whatever is usually paid. Many vocal students realize the need of a general musical training, and seek it through studying the piano and through choir and chorus singing. But the vocal teacher seldom finds time to teach his pupils to read music at sight. This is a serious mistake. The artistic use of the voice is dependent on the possession of a trained ear and a cultured musical taste. Ear training and musical culture are greatly facilitated by a knowledge of the technical basis of the art of music. This latter is best acquired, by the vocal student at any rate, through the study of sight reading.

Sight singing and the rudiments of music are taught to better advantage in class work than in private individual instruction. The class system also secures a great saving of time to the teacher. Every teacher should form a little class in sight reading and choral singing, made up of all his pupils. An hour or an hour and a half each week, devoted by the entire class to the study of sight singing and simple part songs and choruses, would give an ample training to all the pupils in this important branch of the art of music.

Many vocal teachers advise their pupils not to sing in choirs and choruses. There may be some ground for the belief that students are apt to fall into bad vocal habits while singing in the chorus. But this risk is entirely avoided by the teacher having his pupils sing in his own chorus, under his own direction.

Another important feature of the musical education is the hearing of good music artistically performed. Vocal students should be urged to attend the opera and the orchestral concerts. They should become familiar with the different forms of composition by actually hearing the masterpieces of music. Chamber music concerts, song recitals, and oratoric performances,--all are of great advantage to the earnest student. When students attend the opera, or hear the great singers in concerts and recitals, they should listen to the singers' tones, and not wonder how the tones are produced.

Ear Training

No special exercises can be given for the training of the ear. The sense of hearing is developed only by attentive listening. Every vocal student should be urged, and frequently reminded, to form the habit of listening attentively to the tones of all voices and instruments. A highly trained sense of hearing is one of the musician's most valuable gifts. A naturally keen musical ear is of course presupposed in the case of any one desiring to study music. This natural gift must be developed by exercise in the ear's proper function,-- listening to sounds.

Experience in listening to voices is made doubly effective in the training of the ear when the student's attention is called to the salient characteristics of the tones heard. In this regard the two points most important for the student to notice are the intonation and the tone quality.

Absolute correctness of intonation, whether in the voice or in an instrument, can be appreciated only by the possessor of a highly cultivated sense of hearing. Many tones are accepted as being in tune which are heard by a very keen ear to be slightly off the pitch, or untrue to the pitch. This matter of a tone being untrue to the pitch is of great importance to the student of music. Many instruments, when unskilfully played, give out tones of this character. The tones are impure; instead of containing only one pitch, each note shades off into pitches a trifle higher, or lower, or both. This faulty type of tone is illustrated by a piano slightly out of tune. On a single note of this piano one string may have remained in perfect tune, the second may have flatted by the merest fraction of a semitone, and the third by a slightly greater interval. When this note is played it is in one sense not out of tune. Yet its pitch is untrue, and it shades off into a slightly flat note. In the case of many instruments, notably the flute, the clarinet, and the French horn, unskilled performers often play notes of this character. But in these instruments the composite character of the note is vastly more complex than in the piano. A very keen ear is required to appreciate fully the nature of this untrueness to the pitch. But this is exactly the kind of ear the singer must possess, and it can be acquired only by the experience of attentive listening.

The voice is especially liable to produce tones untrue to the pitch. Stiff-throated singers almost invariably exhibit this faulty tendency. An excessive tension of the throat hampers the vocal cords in their adjustments, and the result is an impure tone. This is more often the cause of an artist singing out of tune than a deficiency of the sense of hearing. Many singers "sharp" or "flat" habitually, and are unable to overcome the habit, even though well aware of it. Only a voice entirely free from stiffness can produce tones of absolute correctness and perfect intonation. Du Maurier hit upon a very apt description of pure intonation when he said that Trilby always sang "right into the middle of the note." As an impurity of intonation is almost always an indication of throat tension, vocal teachers should be keenly sensitive to this type of faulty tone.

Tone quality is a subject of surpassing interest to the musician. Whatever may be thought the true purpose of music, there can be no question as to one demand made on each individual instrument,--it must produce tones of sensuous beauty. A composer may delight in dissonances; but no instrument of the orchestra may produce harsh or discordant tones. Of beauty of tone the ear is the sole judge; naturally so, for the only appeal of the individual tone is to the ear. Melody, rhythm, and harmony may appeal to the intellect, but the quality of each component tone is judged only by the ear.

Each instrument has its own characteristic tone quality. The student of singing should become familiar with the sounds of the different orchestral instruments. Attention to this is extremely valuable in the training of the ear.

Beauty of tone was seen to be the truest and best indication of the correct vocal action. The voice has its own tonal beauty, entirely different in character from any artificial instrument. Students of singing should listen for every fine shade of tone quality in the voices of other singers. They should learn to detect the slightest blemish on the quality of every tone, the slightest deviation from the correct pitch.

As the voice is guided by the ear, the first requirement of a singer is a keen sense of hearing. For a keen ear to be of benefit, the student must learn to listen to his own voice. This is not altogether an easy matter. For one to learn to hear oneself justly and correctly requires considerable practice. The singer is placed at a natural disadvantage in listening to himself. This is due to two causes. In the first place, the direct muscular sensations of singing are so complex, and so distributed about the throat and face, that the singer's attention is apt to be divided between these and his auditory sensations. Second, the sound waves are conducted to the ear internally, by the vibration of the bones of the head, as well as externally, by the air waves. The internally conveyed vibrations are a rumbling rather than a true sound; the only true tone is the external sound, heard by the singer in the same way as by a listener. Yet the attention is more apt to be taken up with the internal rumbling than with the external tone. Every vocal student must be taught to listen to himself, to disregard the muscular sensations and the internal rumbling, and to pay attention only to the real tones of his voice.

Throat stiffness greatly increases the difficulty of listening to oneself. Both the muscular sensations and the internal rumbling are heightened by the increased muscular tension. A stiff-throated singer confounds the muscular with the auditory sensations; the feeling of muscular effort also makes him believe his tones to be much more powerful than they really are.

The Acquirement of Skill

Skill in the use of the voice is acquired solely by practice in singing. Only one rule is required for the conduct of vocal practice, that is, that the voice thrives on beautiful sounds. Musical taste must always guide the vocal student in practising. The voice cannot well do more than is demanded by the ear. If a student is unable to distinguish a correct intonation, his voice will not intone correctly. A student must hear and recognize his own faults or there is no possibility of his correcting them. He must be familiar with the characteristics of a perfect musical tone in order to demand this tone of his voice.

In the student's progress the ear always keeps slightly in advance of the voice. Both develop together, but the ear takes the lead. The voice needs practice to enable it to meet the demands of the ear. As this practice goes on day by day the ear in the meantime becomes keener and still more exacting in its demands on the voice.

To train a voice is in reality a very simple matter. Nothing is required of the student but straightforward singing. Provided the student's daily practice of singing be guided by a naturally keen ear and a sound musical taste, the voice will steadily progress. Little need be said here about the technical demands made on the voice in modern music. The standards of vocal technique are well known to all vocal teachers, and indeed to musicians generally. Further, the scope of this work is limited to the basic principle of vocal technique,-- correct tone-production.

For starting the voice properly on the road to the perfect action, intelligently guided practice alone is needed. This practice must be carried on under the direction of a competent teacher. But the teacher cannot pay attention solely to the technical training of the student's voice. As has been seen, the training of the voice is impossible without the cultivation of the sense of hearing; and this is dependent in great measure on the general musical education of the student. The teacher must therefore direct the student's musical education as the basic principle of Voice Culture.

The Avoidance of Throat Stiffness

A great advance will be brought about in the profession of Voice Culture when vocal teachers become thoroughly familiar with the subject of throat stiffness. This is the only troublesome feature of the training of voices. Teachers must be always on the alert to note every indication of throat stiffness. The correction of faults of production has always been recognized as one of the most important elements of vocal training. Faults of production are of two kinds, natural and acquired. Natural faults are exhibited in some degree by every vocal student. These are due solely to the lack of facility in the use of the voice and to the beginner's want of experience in hearing his own voice. Acquired faults develop only as the result of unnatural throat tension. The most common cause of acquired faults of tone-production was seen in the attempt consciously to direct the mechanical operations of the voice.

Equipped with a thorough understanding of the subject of throat stiffness, the teacher is in no danger of permitting his pupils to contract faulty habits of tone-production. Here the great value of the empirical knowledge of the voice is seen. The slightest trace of incipient throat stiffness must be immediately detected by the teacher in the sound of the pupil's tones. To correct the faulty tendency in the beginning is comparatively simple. By listening closely to every tone sung by his pupils in the course of instruction, noting both the musical character of the tones and the sympathetic sensations of throat action, the master will never be in doubt whether a tendency to throat stiffness is shown. In locating the natural faults of production the teacher will also find his empirical knowledge of the voice a most valuable possession.

CHAPTER IX

OUTLINES OF A PRACTICAL METHOD OF VOICE CULTURE

According to the accepted idea of Voice Culture, the word "method" is taken to mean only the plan supposedly followed for imparting a correct manner of tone-production. Owing to the prevalence of the mechanical idea, the acquirement of the correct vocal action has become so difficult as to demand almost the exclusive attention of both teachers and students. Very little time is left for other subjects of vastly more importance. Aside from the matter of tone-production, teachers do not seem to realize the importance, or even the possibility, of systematizing a course of instruction in singing.

Scientific Voice Culture is inconceivable without a systematic plan of procedure. But this is not dependent on a set of rules for imparting the correct vocal action. Eliminating the idea of mechanical vocal management does not imply the abandonment of methodical instruction in singing. On the contrary, Voice Culture cannot be made truly systematic so long as it is based on an erroneous and unscientific theory of vocal management. A vocal teacher cannot perfect a system of instruction until he has done with the mechanical idea. Then he will find himself to be in possession of all the materials of a sound practical method.

Most important of the materials of a practical method is a comprehensive repertoire of vocal music. Every teacher should have at his command a wide range of compositions in every form available for the voice. This should include simple exercises, vocalises with and without words, songs of every description, arias of the lyric, dramatic, and coloratura type, and recitatives, as well as concerted numbers of every description. All these compositions should be graded, according to the difficulties they present, both technical in the vocal sense, and musical. For every stage of a pupil's progress the teacher should know exactly what composition to assign for study.

Every composition used in instruction, be it simple exercise or elaborate aria, should be first of all melodious. For the normally gifted student the sense of melody and the love of singing are almost synonymous. Next to the physical endowments of voice and ear the sense of melody is the vocal student's most important gift. This feeling for melody should be appealed to at every instant. Students should not be permitted to sing anything in a mechanical fashion. Broken scales, "five finger exercises," and mechanical drills of every kind, are altogether objectionable. They blunt the sense of melody, and at the same time they tend to induce throat stiffness. Beauty of tone and of melody should always be the guiding principle in the practice of singing.

All the elements of instruction,--musical education, ear training, and the acquirement of facility in the use of the voice,--can be combined in the singing of melodious compositions. While the teacher should know the precise object of each study, this is not necessary for the student. Have the pupil simply sing his daily studies, with good tone and true musical feeling, and all the rest will take care of itself.

Every vocal teacher will formulate his method of instruction according to his own taste and judgment. There will always be room for the exercise of originality, and for the working out of individual ideas. His own experience, and his judgment in each individual case, must guide the teacher in answering many important questions. Whether to train a voice up or down, whether to pay special attention to enunciation, when to introduce the trill, what form of studies to use for technique and ornament,--these are all matters for the teacher to decide in his own way.

Above all else the teacher should seek to make the study of singing interesting to his pupils. This cannot be done by making the idea of method and of mechanical drudgery prominent. Singing is an art; both teacher and student must love their art or they cannot succeed. Everything the student is called on to do should be a distinct pleasure. To master the piano or the violin many hours of tedious practice are required. Students of singing are indeed fortunate to be spared the necessity of this tiresome work. In place of two or three hours' daily practice of scales and exercises, the vocal student need do nothing but sing good music.

Much is required of a competent vocal teacher. First of all, he must be a cultured musician and a capable judge both of composition and of performance. Further, while not necessarily a great singer, he must have a thorough command of all the resources of his own voice. His understanding of the voice should embrace a fair knowledge of vocal physiology and of vocal psychology. His ear should be so highly trained, and his experience in hearing singers so wide, that he possess in full the empirical knowledge of the voice. The vocal teacher must be familiar with the highest standards of singing. He should hear the great artists of his day and also be well versed in the traditions of his art.

A highly important gift of the vocal teacher is tact. He must know how to deal with his pupils, how to smooth over the rough places of temperament. He should be able to foster a spirit of comradeship among his pupils, to secure the stimulating effect of rivalry, while avoiding the evils of jealousy. Tact is an important element also in individual instruction. Some students will demand to know the reason of everything, others will be content to do as they are told without question. One student may be led to stiffen his throat by instruction which would have no such effect on another. In every case the teacher must study the individual temperaments of his pupils and adapt his method to the character of each student.

Practical instruction, in its outward aspect, should be very simple. At one lesson the teacher assigns certain studies and has the pupil sing them. Now and then the teacher sings a few measures in order to give the student the correct idea of the effects to be obtained. If any pronounced fault is shown in the student's tones, the master calls attention to the fault, perhaps imitating it, to make it more apparent to the student. In his home practice the student sings the assigned studies, trying always to get his tones pure and true. At the next lesson the same studies are again sung, and new compositions given for further study.

A great advantage might be gained by combining three, four, or five students in a class and giving lessons of an hour's time, or even an hour and a half. The students might sing in turn, all the others listening to the one who is singing. This form of instruction would be of great service in ear training, and in acquainting the students with the various qualities of vocal tone, both correct and faulty. Much time would thus be saved in giving explanations and in pointing out the characteristics of tone to be sought or avoided. On the side of musical education, instruction in small classes would also be found very effective.

A thorough understanding of Vocal Science, including both the mechanical features of tone-production and the psychological aspects of singing, is almost indispensable to the vocal teacher. But the student of singing will in most cases derive no benefit from this scientific knowledge. Those students who plan to become teachers must of course study Vocal Science. Yet even these students will do well to defer this study until they have acquired a thorough mastery of their voices.

* * *

Musical progress would seem to have taken a peculiar direction when a voice need be raised in defense of the old art of pure singing. Several famous writers on musical subjects would have us believe that the love of vocal melody is outgrown by one who reaches the heights of musical development. This may be true; but if so, the world has not yet progressed so far. Music without melody may some day be written. But Mozart knew naught of it, nor Beethoven, nor Wagner. Melody is still beautiful, and never more lovely than when artistically sung by a beautiful voice. We have not reached a point where we can afford to toss lightly aside the old art of Bel Canto.

For its future development, if not indeed for its continued existence, the art of singing depends on an improvement in the art of training voices. For this to be accomplished, mechanical methods must be abandoned. If this work succeeds in bringing home to the vocal profession the error of mechanical instruction in singing, it will have served its purpose.

###

Made in the USA
Middletown, DE
09 November 2022

14505015R00099